FOUNDATIONS FOR
A PRACTICAL THEOLOGY
OF MINISTRY

FOUNDATIONS FOR A PRACTICAL THEOLOGY OF MINISTRY

JAMES N. POLING
DONALD E. MILLER

Abingdon Press

Nashville

Foundations for a Practical Theology of Ministry

Copyright © 1985 by Abingdon Press

Library of Congress Cataloging in Publication Data

POLING, JAMES N. (JAMES NEWTON), 1942–
   Foundations for a practical theology of ministry.
   Includes bibliographical references and index.
   1. Theology, Practical. I. Miller, Donald Eugene.
   II. Title.
   BV3.P64   1985   253   84-14529

ISBN 0-687-13340-8

Scripture quotations unless otherwise noted are from the Revised Standard
Version of the Bible, copyrighted 1946, 1952, 1971, © 1973, by the Division of
Christian Education of the National Council of the Churches of Christ in the
U.S.A., and used by permission.

Excerpts from "Pastoral Theology in a Pluralistic Age" by Don S. Browning,
excerpts from "The Foundations of Practical Theology: Meaning, Action,
Self" by Thomas W. Ogletree, excerpts from "Toward a Theology of
Rhetoric/Preaching" by Leander E. Keck, and excerpts from "Practical
Theology and the Shaping of Christian Lives" by James W. Fowler from
Practical Theology, the Emerging Field in Theology, Church, and World.
Edited, with an Introduction, by Don S. Browning. Copyright © 1983 by Don
S. Browning. Reprinted by permission of Harper & Row, Publishers, Inc.

The material in chapter 2 "Types of Practical Theology" appeared in similar
form in the Spring 1984 issue of *Theological Education.*

Excerpts from the article "The Future of Pastoral Theology," by Rodney
Hunter, *Pastoral Psychology,* Fall, 1980, are copyright © 1980 by Human
Sciences Press, 72 Fifth Avenue, N.Y., N.Y. 10011.

Lewis Mudge has given permission to quote material from his manuscripts in
the Seminar in Practical Theology and from his conversations with the
authors.

MANUFACTURED BY THE PARTHENON PRESS AT
NASHVILLE, TENNESSEE, UNITED STATES OF AMERICA

To Newton and Virginia Poling
who taught me the meaning of ministry

To Daniel and Catherine Coning
who helped me experience the
church as a living community

Contents

ONE   Introduction: The Faith Community
and Theological Interpretation........... 9

TWO   Types of Practical Theology.................... 29

THREE   A Method for Practical Theology............62

FOUR   Guidelines for the Practice of Ministry... 100

FIVE   Community Formation as the Task of
Ministry...................................... 126

SIX   The Challenge to Ministry Education..... 147

Notes and References.........................171

Index...184

Introduction:
The Faith Community
and Theological Interpretation

The focus of this book is living Christian community. The heart of Christian life for the individual is shared life with other believers. This shared life includes patterns of interaction with common meanings which are understood theologically. That is, the church is a community which is constantly interpreting its life within its ongoing relationship with God. The disciplines of theology have developed over many years as the history of the church's interpretation of its life. As theology has adopted the methods of scientific investigation, it has divided into various sub-specialties which are often highly technical in linguistic, historical, and philosophical analysis, and one of its difficulties is trying to bridge the gap between its insights and the daily life of the faithful. Through the disciplines of theology, we know much about Christian communities of the past and their attempts to be faithful, but such study is often so embedded in technical language that it seems abstract and far removed from the praxis of local communities of faith. At the same time, the pressure for action and solving immediate problems within living communities of faith often seems to prevent deliberate and disciplined reflection about its continuity with the tradition. Often Scriptures are used unreflectively and assumptions are made about the truth of the gospel which are unexamined. Ongoing life in Christian community is frequently in danger of losing its center in faith and accommodating to the surrounding culture to the extent of confusing its identity. In this book, we want to explore the nature of living Christian community including theological interpretation of its shared life in the world and to explore the contribution of the disciplines of theology to Christian life.[1]

Practical theology is one way of talking about the relationship of living Christian community and theological interpretation. From Aquinas until the Enlightenment, practical theology was understood to be the application of the first principles of reason to experience.[2] The mind, for Aquinas, understands the fundamental principles of reason. The conscience links perception, will, and reason so that an inclination to act in a certain way follows from rightly perceiving a situation in relation to rightly understanding basic principles of ethics. For generations, practical theology moved from basic theological principles to application. The skepticism of Hume and the Enlightenment broke the easy link of theological understanding and application. In its place arose the many modern empirical sciences that attempt to make sense of experience.

The ultimate rational unity of the many empirically based sciences is problematic. Practical theology as a unified discipline was consequently largely abandoned. In its place arose the various practical disciplines of ministry which were guided largely by one or another empirical science. The result is that practical theology has been replaced by a series of practical ministerial disciplines.

It is becoming evident that the multiplication of practical disciplines oriented to empirical methodologies is without end, and that ministry is in danger of losing its center in the effort to be multi-competent. Therefore, we join with those who are calling for a revival of a discipline of practical theology. Such a new discipline can share with the older discipline a concern about the fundamental beliefs and teachings of the tradition. Unlike the older discipline, practical theology in our day must also attend to the empirical sciences. However, that attention can occur in an ongoing and living dialogue that keeps its center in a community-embedded belief in Jesus Christ. Our effort here is to forward such a newly conceived discipline of practical theology.[3]

Two definitions guide the focus of this book. First, we define Christian community as a process of interaction among believers who seek to be faithful to Jesus Christ as revealed in Scripture and its tradition. We want to understand how context, structures, and dynamics affect this shared life and how the community sustains its continuity with other communities who also confess Christ. Second, we define practical theology as reflection arising out of the living experiences of communities of faith and resulting in faith-informed interpretations that serve to guide the ongoing life and actions of those communities. (See chapter 3 for a fuller definition of practical theology.) We want to understand the hermeneutical process of moving from shared experiences to abstract theological concepts that actually guide ongoing praxis of the community in its mission to the world.

We believe that community is an emerging metaphor for Christian life which has potential for unifying many other conceptions. For example, servanthood has been an image that has been meaningful and useful to many as a way to understand ministry in the church and mission in the world. Jesus said that he "came not to be served, but to serve" (Matt. 20:28). But to what end does servanthood aim? To the end that God's "beloved

11

community"[4] be established for all. Servanthood is a partial image for faith, a reminder that the formation of Christian community requires a facilitative style that is not hierarchical and authoritarian, but inclusive and self-critical. Another image of faithfulness is discipleship. Christians are called to be obedient to a living Lord who sometimes requires risk and action in a direction that one does not fully understand. Discipleship enables communities to follow their Lord when the pragmatic consequences are not evident. For formation of God's kingdom[5] often requires sacrifice of immediate goals and commitment to a greater good that cannot easily be imagined. We are called to live as disciples to the One who is creating a universe of peace and justice for all. Thus, community is the more inclusive image for both servanthood and discipleship as images. God is creating a "beloved community" which includes all persons regardless of their wealth and social status and which has no place for violence or oppression. The church is called to be God's community as a sign of the future redemption of all creation. Ministry is faithful leadership which works to form God's community for all persons. Part of the emphasis of this book is the development of community as a metaphor for understanding God's action in the world.

A crucial aspect of Christian community is theological interpretation. Theology is practical when it enables the living community to reflect upon and guide its own action in the context of God's continuing action. A part of life in the community of faith is an ongoing process of interpretation of its experience and story in relation to the larger story of God's action in Scripture and through history, into the present and into the future. "What is God doing among us?" and "What is God calling us to become?" are key questions of practical theology. Responding to these questions requires awareness of

12

Scripture and the tradition of interpretation: What was God doing in the law and the prophets and in the life, death, and resurrection of Jesus Christ? Full and responsible answers to these questions are complex, so the church has called specialists to study the tradition. One result has been the development of disciplines of theology which often seem to be autonomous and separated from the church. At the same time, the pressures within the life of the church for immediate action seem to deny the possibility of careful reflection and interpretation. A gap between life within community and the specialized theological disciplines has frequently developed. Sometimes the gap is so exaggerated that theology as a discipline and life within Christian community seem to be unrelated to one another. At other times, these two realms seem to complement and support each other.

It is a thesis of this book that theological interpretation belongs to Christian community as a constitutive dimension. Without theological interpretation, Christian community loses its vitality and vision. Without community, theology loses its locus and power. We believe that recent changes in the church and in the nature of theology have again revealed their intrinsic relationship to one another. In the discussion that follows, we hope to describe in a more nearly appropriate and adequate way the relationship between community process and theological interpretation. Such a description is essential for religious leadership. The task of Christian religious leadership is to engage the community of faith in a process of interpretation and formation of its shared life and thought in ways that express the vitality of the Christian tradition and lead to transformation of the world. The mission of Christian community is a shared praxis which brings God's liberation to all creation.[6]

Changes in the Church

Anyone who is active at any level of church life surely senses both excitement and anxiety. Parts of the church are involved in confrontation with political powers about nuclear war and social justice in ways that may affect the future of the globe. Other parts of the church are engaged with indigenous groups of Christians all over the world as a result of aggressive evangelistic programs. In local congregations, Christians are involved in study and conflict about various expressions of faith and Christian ethics. Often the church seems divided against itself and impotent in the face of secular powers. We suggest that this excitement and anxiety is an expression of the church in transition. In many places the church is changing from a largely uniform membership with fairly clear beliefs and ethics to a more pluralistic, diverse, and decentralized collection of communities. Some of the roots of this shift can be traced to the Protestant Reformation, especially as it has been expressed in the American democratic tradition and economic individualism. The shift to a more pluralistic, decentralized ecclesiology has possibilities of disintegration and division as well as enormous creativity.

In some ways the church has seldom been so alive. Both liberal and evangelical wings of the American church are responding to the cries of the poor and oppressed in the world. There is great debate and deep disagreement over strategies and theology of mission, but the potential for genuine engagement with the poor of the world is a real possibility in some places. Increased exposure to the oppressed and hungry world has led the church at many levels to reexamine the social location of much theological reflection. Theology itself is not a neutral enterprise, but reflects the perspective of the communities in which it takes place. Identification with the poor often challenges the traditional methods and content of theology. The Scriptures mean something much different from the perspective of base communities in Latin America. Dialogue between Christians in the U.S. and the Third World has resulted in significant questions, primarily the tendency of privilege to dictate a community's faith. There is excitement about the new possibilities for awareness of how socioeconomic class limits the vision of particular communities and blinds them to the larger vision of God's love and peace.[7] At the same time, the debate threatens to divide Christians from one another at the deepest levels.

Another sign of excitement in the church is a deepened search for the biblical and theological roots of the faith. In all traditions and locations, Christians are engaged in Bible study and intense discussion to discover the meaning of the Christian life. Persons want to know what the Bible says about the role of women as church leaders, the essence of marriage and family life amid the brokenness of divorce, the ethics of sexuality, abortion, gun control, violence, peace. Christians at many local levels are ignoring traditional denominational differences and are uniting on a variety of projects. The doctrinal issues that divided Christians in the past are often being ignored in favor of joint mission and prayers for peace. In many ways, local churches are ahead of their national leaders and theologians in finding forms of ecumenical cooperation. At all levels of the church's life, there is excitement about the Christian faith and its relevance in a changing world.

Some writers have suggested that the renewed study and debate are partly the result of the collapse of traditional authorities.[8] In traditions that have de-

15

pended on clear biblical authority, the discoveries of the pluralism and historicity of biblical texts have often been disturbing. Some hold to a doctrine of biblical inerrancy as a defense against recent scholarly discoveries. Some have lost faith in the Bible as a relevant document for modern times because their particular interpretations have been questioned. In between these extremes are the many Christians who struggle to interpret the Bible with careful regard for its culturally conditioned context but without losing its authority as a rule for faith and practice. Other traditions have depended on the undisputed authority of church leadership to provide the inspired interpretation of the tradition. But these traditions have experienced doubts about their authority because of the conflicting experiences at the local level. When church leaders take rigid ethical positions on such issues as abortion, divorce, homosexuality, and others, then Christian families that experience brokenness around these issues feel caught. Should they be faithful to the interpretations of the church leaders, or faithful to the fabric that seems to hold their families together? Where there is a loss of faith in the inerrancy of the Bible or church leaders, the collapse of such authority results in conflict within Christian communities. This shift results in confusion and fear, but it also opens up the possibility that local communities of faith can begin thinking theologically in relation to their own experiences.

Another source of anxiety in the church is the perceived loss of consensus on important issues of faith and value. As the church changes, as traditional authorities seem fallible, as local communities begin to do their own faith reflection, so the differences between sincere people of faith become apparent. Increased freedom of belief and behavior can enrich community life with diversity, but the lack of consensus can threaten the very fabric of community itself. What does hold community life together? At some level a community must have agreement about values or images of meaning or covenants of purpose. In the past, communities tended to be homogeneous in culture, theology, and values. Now, increasingly, Christian communities are pluralistic.[9] The result is that persons must confront one another in order to work out their differences and develop an understanding that creates a web of relationships. For example, divorce is a difficult issue for any face-to-face community. The brokenness between persons disrupts the relational fabric so that often one or both of the marriage partners leaves the community. Divorce also disrupts a theology and ethics based on love and reconciliation and covenant. Rigid ethical positions seldom help community process because they overlook the bonding between persons that is deeper than thinking. More helpful is for a community to work through the brokenness with all persons concerned and to allow the emergence of new relationships that promise to preserve the integrity of the individual persons as well as of the community itself. Failure to stay in conversation until a new understanding is reached can threaten the very existence of a particular community. How can a local community of faith flourish when it has basic disagreements on such issues as divorce, biblical authority, and mission?

One response to the threat of pluralism is the development of rigid and authoritarian structures and leadership that enforces conformity in thought and behavior. Recent growth of some fundamentalist groups and various cults may in part be a response to the anxiety of pluralism and its implicit threat to traditional community life. However, we believe that the changes in the church also present opportunities for growth in Christian understanding. Some will feel the threat of pluralism and the collapse of certain kinds of authority, and will lean toward defensive communities that are closed to the future. Yet, there is also the possibility that local Christian communities can become a source of power for Christian life in the future.

As local Christian communities become enlivened by the Spirit of God through struggles with one another and with the difficult issues of being Christian in the modern world, there is potential for release of tremendous creativity. For this to happen, we need images of the Christian life that can sustain local communities in the midst of anxiety, giving them support to engage in the dialogue that will result in a practical theology for our time.

The task is risky and complex, but the potential rewards at all levels are tremendous. There is opportunity for a new sense of power and vitality in the Christian church from its priests to lay study groups. The metaphor of community may help provide a center for understanding the excitement and anxiety of Christian life in the modern world.

Changes in the Guiding Vision of Ministry

In order for local communities of faith to engage in doing practical theology, pastors and other leaders will need a new vision of their roles. A variety of images of pastoral leadership is operative in the church: theologian, educator (teaching elder), pastoral director, counselor, preacher, administrator. Each of these images has an important aspect of ministry at its root. Certainly, a pastor should be one who is committed to the Christian tradition and can make the Scriptures come alive for the people in the role of teacher and preacher. A pastor should be one who is sensitive to the various needs of persons and families and can respond personally and professionally to them. A pastor should be able to direct and administer a complex program of nurture and outreach that involves as many persons as possible in the congregation's mission. In the past decades, each of these aspects of ministry has received careful attention and, in some cases, has spawned a sub-discipline of its own.[10] Such research and training has deepened the church's understanding of the various aspects of the Christian life.

However, one of the problematic consequences of these various images is the disintegration of the central guiding images of ministry and the consequent fragmentation of ministerial practice. Theological education has come to be organized around competing understandings of the center of ministry: preaching, education, counseling, administration. Many pastors yearn to become specialists in one or another of these sub-disciplines as a way of establishing clear competence. Pastors tend to specialize in one of an imposing variety of competencies: preaching, teaching, counseling, administration, social action, lay education, theology. Such specialization springs from a particular professional view of ministry.

Edward Farley has described the difficulties of the professionalized ministry.[11] A professional is one who has a specialized expertise that can be delivered to a client population for monetary return. The secular models are medicine, law, and mental health services. When someone has a problem for which such expertise is appropriate, that person becomes a client and offers payment to the professional for his/her expertise. As ministry accepts a professional model as its primary image, the pastor becomes an expert who has individuals and congregations for clients. In exchange for fees of service or contracts, the pastor delivers that expertise

19

for use by the client. Such a view may clarify what has in the past often been an ambiguous relationship between pastor and congregation.

We are not unhappy with many of the gains in the competence of church leadership and human care that have come through specialization and professionalization. Certainly the profession of ministry has improved skills in teaching, preaching, counseling, and administration. But the danger facing ministry is the loss of its center, its integrity. What is the difference between specialized ministries and their secular counterparts outside the church? What is Christian about ministry when its guiding images come from the professions in the surrounding society? The gains in competence that develop by moving toward professionalization of its ministry may come at the cost of the integrity of ministry.

In this book we lend our support to those who are calling for a renewal of the integration of ministry. We believe that the current tendencies toward specialization and professionalization threaten the integrity of ministry. Each of the various specialties is based on a partial image that needs a larger image in order to be coherent and adequate. Preaching rests on the community's need to be addressed by the tradition, inspired, and motivated to be faithful to its vision. Education stands within the community's need to be theologically articulate about its tradition and its present experiences. Counseling assumes the community's need to be sensitive and responsive to the deep pain of persons within its fellowship and in the neighborhood. Administration shapes the community's need to be organized in its nurture and mission and clear about its goals. While all such activities are appropriate individual aspects of the responsibility of ministry, we propose that the unifying image for ministry is its focus upon the

20

community of faith. Ministry is leadership that is called and trained to serve the community of faith in its local activities, in its ecumenical relationships, and in its outreach in the world. In order to fulfill the function of community formation, ministry needs a variety of skills in communication, administration, counseling, worship, social action, evangelism, education, international relations, peacemaking, and others. In its role of forming community, ministry will be called on to do many things, among which must always be included theological interpretation of its life in the world.

The concept of community formation may provide the larger image of ministry which reveals the proper role of the various specialties, that is, the role of serving the formation of Christian community in its mission in the world. In fact, we suggest that when ministry begins to understand its center to be community formation rather than professional expertise or some other image, then ministry may become a model for secular professions in our day. Perhaps an appropriate image for medicine and counseling is not primarily its professional expertise, but rather its role in forming a community that is physically and mentally healthy. The appropriate role for law may not be primarily its ability to win cases, but rather its responsibility for a legal structure that is fair and adequate for the whole community. It may eventually become clear that while professional skill is needed in every society, an appropriate image for all professions is not primarily expert and client, but responsibility for community formation. That is, trained leadership is called to serve the total community in its formation so as to include all its members while being active in its particular mission in the larger world. If the church can forge this move in its own life, the new awareness may have implications for other forms of community life.

21

Changes in Theology

New ideas about the nature of biblical interpretation, the importance of local particular expressions of faith, shifting views of language and its relation to experience, and the need for theology to become more practical have opened up the question of the nature of the theological task.

Research on the relation of biblical texts to the communities that produced and interpreted them is changing the assumptions about Bible study.[12] Rather than search for a single, true interpretation of the Bible for all times, scholars are asking what a particular text meant in a particular community and how that meaning changes as the community context changes. This style of interpretations has led to important discoveries about the relation of classical texts and particular communities.[13] Every text is particular in its origin. That is, it arises within a particular community to serve a particular need. The effects of a classical text are not limited to its origin, but include potential revelation for other communities about the nature of reality and the action of God. The meaning of a text can transcend its original context and become relevant and useful for other communities with different traditions in other times and places. Some biblical scholars have shown how the same text has come to mean different things to other communities in other times.[14] One result of such a hermeneutic is a shift of interest from the universal to the particular, with ensuing respect for particular traditions. In other words, particular texts can have much larger meanings than the original context suggests. Classical texts are those texts that seem to point to universal values and images that have significance to any community willing to become engaged in conversation with them.[15]

The shift to interest in the particular in theology has meant a new respect for the experiences of dispossessed and oppressed groups. If particular expressions of the Christian tradition potentially have as much validity as those expressions that have received public attention and want to claim universality, then research should focus on the forgotten or suppressed texts and communities that produced them.[16] One result of such recent research is the discovery that experiences of oppression do lead to alternate views of faith that have validity, and often directly challenge the dominant interpretations of the faith. Base communities in Latin America are interpreting the Scripture in the light of their experiences of being exploited and dominated by oppressive social structures. Their work is showing that certain ways of understanding the Christian faith by privileged groups tends to privitize the biblical texts and underestimate the radical social implications of Jesus' words on justice and the imminent kingdom.[17] Likewise, study of the Bible by American blacks and women who are conscious of the oppressive social structures for these groups is revealing new insights into the nature of God and God's relationships with humanity.[18]

One clear conclusion from liberation theology is that religion is almost always co-opted by the dominant culture and domesticated so that it serves the limited social interests of the privileged. The irony of such acculturation for Christians is that the Bible was written almost totally within a context of oppression in which the images of change had revolutionary implications and which assumed a deeply corporate sense of belonging to God and to one another.[19] The shift in biblical hermeneutics toward an interest in particular expressions of faith is leading to new interpretations of the Christian tradition. One implication of this hermeneutic is that local communities of faith should be encouraged to engage in their own theological reflection with particular attention to the social location of their experiences rather than passively accepting an imported theology whose location and interests may be completely different. An adequate interpretation of the Scriptures in any particular community of faith can be done only within that particular context.

A corresponding change in theology is the shifting view of language. For most of history, language was seen as a mirror of reality. It was generally believed that specific words corresponded to human experiences and enabled persons to communicate with one another. There was a perceived one-to-one correspondence between language and experience. For example, "person" is a word to which the variety of people correspond, and we can recognize a person because we have a word and an idea that corresponds to this experience. Because such words are common within a culture, the people in that culture can communicate meaningfully with one another.

However, the relation of language and experience is now being described in more complex terms. Language is less a mirror of reality than a series of metaphors about reality, and no particular linguistic expression corresponds exactly with any experience. Rather, particular expressions create images of experience that bring certain aspects into focus and relegate other aspects to the background. Language is necessary in order to organize experience, but it always organizes experience so that the images partially disclose and partially hide the full depth and complexity of experience.[20]

For example, the metaphor of discipleship is an image of the Christian life that highlights the receptive and dependent aspects of one's relationship with God. It is valuable because it emphasizes the role of believer as follower and child, an appropriate way to understand one aspect of Christian faith. However, discipleship tends to hide from view the part of the biblical tradition that invites the faithful into partnership, co-creation, struggle, and even wrestling with God. Discipleship as an image may lead the community into agreement in thought and action on moral issues, but it may mislead the community in areas where ambiguity and hidden conflict are important ingredients.

Discovery of the metaphorical nature of language helps us see the value and the limitations of various linguistic expressions, and it may free us from a correspondence view that can function in authoritarian ways that undermine full participation in community process. Part of the task of theology is to uncover the metaphors that enable communities to draw on the tradition in such a way that the present is transformed and God's action is revealed. Such a view requires careful attention to the particular social and historical context of all language and the experiences it seeks to describe. A goal of theology is to discover the Christian metaphors that enliven community life and release the creativity of persons in their interaction with God.

Practical theology is one way to focus our attention on the reality of community process and the function of theological interpretation as a part of that process. The changing self-definition of theology opens up some new possibilities which have been impossible in the past. Interpreting the Scriptures in terms of their particular language, culture, and socio-political context gives us new images of the nature of God and of God's relationship to the faithful communities. Having a deeper respect for the particular experiences of contemporary living, Christian communities gives us new ways of understanding our shared life. We believe that the time has come when a newly conceived practical theology which is centered in its continuity with the tradition and yet is deeply embedded in the empirical life of living comunities is possible. We join with those who are calling for a practical theology that is not primarily the science of studying the Bible and developing coherent propositions about God, the world, and appropriate ethical responses, but is directed to the goal of faithful and transforming action by the church in the world.[21] We call for a practical theology that is not primarily a science about faith, but is the development of theological understandings that are appropriate to the ongoing life of particular faith communities. We believe that theological reflection arises when the faithful community tries to relate its current experiences in the world as they are interpreted by cultural metaphors to the tradition of believing communities in the past. Such theological reflection leads to interpretations of the tradition that guide the community in transforming action.

This book presents one way of doing practical theology. It is directed to leaders of the church who want to think more deeply about the nature of Christian community and the role of theological interpretation in its everyday life. We expect that this book will be helpful to theological educators who are responsible for ministry training. We hope that this work will be a helpful contribution to the debate within theology about its practical task in the shared life of Christian communities.

Chapter 2 is a summary of some of the issues that are being debated in practical theology. Two parts of this discussion are highlighted here. First is the question of the method of correlating the biblical tradition with cultural interpretations of contemporary experience. There are various suggestions for adequate interdisciplinary dialogue. Second is the tension within theology between uncovering the universal values that guide the formation of society and identifying the particular theologies that emerge in living communities as they interact in the world. We attempt to describe six types of practical theology in the current scene.

Chapter 3 describes our method of practical theology. We outline certain assumptions about the nature of community and the nature of theology and then develop a sequence of six steps that we believe takes the various issues into account. There are several dangers in doing practical theology. One danger is that community life will be understood simplistically and that theological abstractions will be based on a superficial understanding of a particular community and its social and historical context. Special care must be taken to develop appropriate sensitivities to community experiences. Communities of faith are complex events with hidden and latent patterns of meaning that must be uncovered with empathy and self-awareness. A second danger is that the everyday pressure of community life for action will short-circuit the time and discipline needed for adequate understanding and appropriation of the tradition. There are many examples where communities have been formed by biblical understandings which cannot be supported by study of the actual texts. If Christians are a people whose identity is continuous with God's people of previous generations, then we must be thoughtful about our past and its application to the present.

Chapter 4 illustrates our method through examples from the life of actual congregations. Practical theology can be described as a rational method, but its embodiment in community life cannot be imposed. There is an art and a sensitivity in ministry which involves deep awareness of the context, acceptance of the values and limitations of one's leadership style, and patience in building covenants of commitment and purpose.

Chapter 5 explores the metaphor of community. Any metaphor can be flat and shallow. For some, community means superficial unity and lack of conflict. We suggest that community can be a metaphor of power only if it can account for the several levels of action and thought that make up the complexity of shared life.

Chapter 6 is a manifesto for theological education. If changes in the relation of community and theology are going to come about, theological education will have to be reconsidered. The church will be able to seize the opportunities of our time only with committed and well-trained leadership. The abstraction of thelogy and the disengagement of leaders from community life are reflected and perpetuated in theological education more than any other place. Unless the seminaries and other schools can focus their theological perception on the real action of living communities, theology will continue to be abstract and ministry impotent.

This book is also dedicated to the contemporary church and its leadership. Even though the church often seems divided and impotent in relation to the modern crises of personal meaning and global survival, we believe that the struggle to be faithful within Christian community is the most appropriate response. Out of the church can come the vision and values that will transform the world. We pray for God's power and wisdom as we search out God's truth for our generation.

Types of Practical Theology

If we are to recover a genuine practical theology, we must attend to the many ways the term "practical theology" is used in different settings. Various specialists in ministry skills use practical theology as a way to rediscover the theological roots of their work. Systematic theologians also employ practical theology as a way to take account of the pluralism of perspectives and the relativity of ethical norms in modern society. Theological educators utilize practical theology as a way to integrate the disciplines of theology and the skill areas of the seminary curriculum. Finally, some liberationists cite practical theology as a way of referring to the importance of *praxis* for modern theology.

The new discovery of the term "practical theology," however, does not imply an underlying convergence of interests among these specialties. Each interest may have polemical reasons for the use of this term which would belie any attempts to describe a coherent form of theology. There is, in fact, no stated consensus that includes all of these specialists' concerns. Yet perhaps there exists a deeper spirit of unity in the discussion that has not yet been discovered. If so, such a coherence must be based on mutual acceptance of a form of

29

theology commonly called "practical theology." If such a theological construct exists, what is its definition, its essential components, and its method?

That there is something called practical theology, a definable discipline, is more than a hunch. Persons with different reasons for being interested in practical theology have significant areas of agreement, even though these agreements are hidden by the varieties of perspectives and symbols they use. Despite the variations in specialists' theological language we can articulate the areas of agreement. There are critical questions not only about definition, but also about the various forms that practical theology can take. Dialogue between theologians becomes productive if these questions are identified and clarified.

This chapter attempts to develop a typology that can organize our thinking and stimulate discussion about the critical issues of practical theology.[1] Such a typology is based on the assumption that there are several valid ways of perceiving the discipline of practical theology to which we can each turn as we face different problems in a variety of contexts. Such types would not identify individual scholars or practitioners, but they identify the types of practical theology that are available. We can assume that each type has validity within some context, and we must be aware that each type has inherent limits. While no typology is adequate to the richness of thought and experience, emphasizing some questions over others, as it necessarily must, practical theology includes these beginning steps toward a typology that will help the community develop a more adequate means of perceiving the field. Such a typology will strengthen our work together, increasing the influence of practical theology in the church and the society.

We are using the concept of ideal type in the same sense as did Max Weber. Human action is a continuum in which there are no obvious seams. To project a type with certain characteristics highlighted gives one an orientation within the continuum of action, and it allows one to see the relationships between types. The types are as reflective of the interests of the observer as they are of what is there in the data. Nevertheless, they give an access to the data that one would not otherwise have. Weber argued that since human action is in its center conceptual, ideal types get closer to human action than the typologies of the physical sciences can get to physical reality.[2]

The ideal types of practical theology revolve around two axes. The first axis is the critical method which is used to bring together the various interpretations available in the Christian tradition and the culture. The second axis is the relationship between church and society. The relationship between church and society can be described as the social horizon and context of the locus of praxis.

The first axis describes the critical method used to bring together a variety of interpretations into some normative unity. In this typology, there are three types of critical methods along a continuum: (1) there is a critical scientific method in which a secular discipline provides the framework and norms for practical theology and the tradition plays a secondary role; (2) there is a critical correlational method which aims at a collaborative dialogue between the Christian tradition and secular disciplines in which each can challenge the other and contribute both descriptive and normative statements, coming to a deeper understanding through their essentially equal dialogue; and (3) there is a critical confessional method in which the Christian tradition is normatively prior, the hermeneutics for its interpretation is of primary importance, and the secular sciences are used cautiously in order to minimize the influence of norms alien to the Christian tradition.

To summarize, there are three types of methods: critical scientific, critical correlational, and critical confessional, on the critical method axis. The word "critical" distinguishes these types from those which are uncritical or precritical in method. On the one hand, there is the extreme in ministry practice which is so dominated by action that there is no time for self-critical reflection and the result is contradiction and incoherence. Similarly, an extreme in fundamentalist theology may be so committed to a certain ideological interpretation of the tradition that it cannot afford to be self-critical. "Critical" implies awareness of one's method and presuppositions, and the definition includes the willingness to revise one's perspective under certain conditions. While there are examples of uncritical types in theology today, they are excluded from this typology in order to describe the valid types that have a legitimate place in this discussion.

The level of criticism just described is that of becoming aware of one's method and presuppositions. Such criticism can occur at the intellectual level, the level of intellectual intuition. However, Kant, Hegel, Marx, Nietzsche, and Freud introduced another level to the meaning of criticism. Kant sought to show how the process of knowing shapes what is known. Hegel argued that knowing occurs as a transcendental dialectic of the spirit. Marx took Hegel's transcendental dialectic and placed it in the material interests of the world, especially class interests. He thereby showed how a perspective can be shaped by material interests in ways not known to the knower. What Marx did for community awareness, Freud did for individual awareness, showing that individuals are often motivated by unconscious motives and interests that are primarily sexual. Nietzsche saw unconscious motives and interests as primarily a drive for power. Since the intellectual development from

Kant to Freud, criticism has included the effort to become aware of unconscious, sexual, economic, and power interests and motives. For example, when theology remains unaware of overwhelming poverty in the world, then it supports oppression of the poor. Post-Kantian criticism attempts to uncover the very social and psychological forces and influences that shape the process of knowing.[3]

In addition, we assume that practical theology does not describe everything that a Christian individual or a community does to be faithful. Practical theology is not the same as practice and the precritical thinking that goes into much practice. Rather, practical theology describes the critical reflection that is done about the meaning of faith and action in the world, and the deposit of that critical reflection in the form of coherent theological statements.

The second axis describes the relationship of church and society. Again, this forms a continuum rather than discontinuous types. Both ends of the continuum are deeply concerned both about the church and about society in general. This axis is not a distinction between church and society, but between various ways of characterizing their relationship. On one end of the continuum, the focus is on the church as a concrete group in its struggle to be faithful in the modern world. The church may or may not be effective in influencing society. Whatever its influence, its purpose is to be centered as a community in a shared practice of life together and to be in mission to the world as a healing influence. At the other end of the continuum, the focus is on the church in its responsibility to society. The mission of the church is to enrich and transform the social order by becoming a part of the public dialogue. The church must be active in presenting its perspective in the public arena and it risks its identity for the sake of the world. The church must judge itself by its effectiveness in social enrichment rather than its shared practice as a community.

The axis of the relationship between church and society is the axis of the horizon of praxis. In this axis neither church nor society is excluded in any of the types. The fundamental question is, Is praxis located primarily in the horizon of religious community or of the secular community? Some would argue that the more fundamental question is that of the conception of religion to the society at large. Troeltsch seemed to argue this latter view in his *Social Teaching of the Christian Churches*. However, a critical understanding of any ideal of religion must show it within the horizon of its praxis. Marxist criticism of the churches would show them to be captive to the economic class structure. Weberian criticism shows the church to be the source of new economic interests in society. Troeltsch was influenced enough by the sociology of knowledge that he did not move directly from a conception of religion to a vision of society. For Troeltsch the conception of religion moves through the horizon of praxis. Hence, it is appropriate to consider practical theologies as primarily oriented to church or to society, while at the same time excluding those views that are oriented only to church or only to society.

Combining these two axes results in six types of practical theology. Each of the critical methods focuses either on facilitating the church's faithfulness and identity, or encouraging the church's dialogue with society. Whether the focus is on the identity of the church or on the effectiveness of the church, there is continuity of method between the types that share a common method.

Any of the critical methods can give priority to formation of the church or formation of society.

We move now to a discussion of each of the six ideal types. It is imperative to perceive these types not as mutually exclusive and competitive with one another, but as following along a continuum described in other terms. To the extent that we fail in this effort, the typology will be less helpful because it tends to oversimplify the work of any one individual in practical theology. Indeed, each of the types may be valid and useful depending on the context. Each of the types has value in certain contexts and limitations in other contexts. We seek to find the validity and limitations of each of the types and to avoid making judgments among them. All of us may use several of the types of practical theology if we see them in this way. Their utility to us will simply depend on our goals, context, and resources. This view of the typology may reduce the temptation to search futilely for the most adequate type for all times and places.

Inevitably, practical theologians will have a preference for one or another type even though one may use several types for various purposes. The reader will find that the authors locate themselves in the confessional and dialogical types and have a preference for focus on the concrete community of the church in its mission within the wider culture. However, we obviously need those who specialize primarily in a careful study of the tradition and its confession as well as those who dedicate their lives to uncovering the theological implications of the various cultural theories. We also need those whose careers are located in the wider public debate about values. The authors' preferences will become more evident as we proceed.

The discussion of these ideal types revolves around three questions:

1. What is the relation of practical theology to philosophy and science?
2. What is the relation of practical theology to the Christian story and tradition?
3. What is the relation of practical theology to the Christian church in its ideal and institutional forms?

Type IA. Practical theology can take the form of a critical science whose purpose is the formation of society.

The norms and methods this science employs come from a scientific discipline with only minor influence from Christian tradition. So understood, practical theology includes certain specialists who were nurtured by the church but now are involved in secular employment, and certain scholars who have chosen to study the church as a social reality, employing scientific methods.

What characteristics constitute the complexion of Type IA? Many persons highly trained in scientific discipline move from church employment into secular employment. Counselors move into mental health agencies and social work agencies. Executives and fund raisers move into business and industry. There are hundreds of persons with theological training in key spots in social agencies who understand their profession as a faith decision and who continue to be interested in theological reflection. Because of the lack of centers for dialogue, such persons often do not produce scholarly material for the church. However, there are conferences sponsored by the church for such persons to gather specifically for discussion of theology and ethics. The Church of the Brethren recently held a well-attended conference on health professions. Its purpose was to discuss American health care in relation to the Christian tradition. For the participants, medical science determines the daily structure and strategies of their work, but they are interested in discussion of the Christian tradition as it informs their work.

Social scientists who are interested in the church as a social reality to be studied also fit into this type. Their focus is not on the formation and mission of the church, but on understanding personality and social institutions generally by studying the church and its members. Certain sub-disciplines specialize in this work—psychology of religion, sociology of religion. Practitioners of these disciplines employ norms and methods that come from science. In fact, such scientists often pride themselves on the use of "hard data" rather than the "soft data" the church usually generates. While they share the church's focus on insight into humanity, their goal is a general knowledge of human nature rather than strategies of church development. These social science disciplines have been influential in some parts of the church, and may have made constructive contributions to the development of theology itself.

A given liberation theology may be Type IA or IB, depending on whether the church or the larger society is the primary point of analysis. Some consider that liberation theology in Latin America, for example, is seeking a social revolution and simply analyzes the manner in which the church has stood in the way. Others see social criticism being put to the service of the church. Likewise, H. Richard Niebuhr's *Social Sources of Denominationalism* analyzed the church in America primarily from the point of view of economic and social theory (Type IA). It was when he wrote a second book entitled *The Kingdom of God in America,* that he moved into a dialogue with the Christian tradition (Type IIA).

In summary, Type IA obtains its norms and strategies from science, perceiving the role of the Christian tradition as secondary. The tradition provides resources for theological reflection as well as data for study. The tradition may provide private motivation and personal support, but it does not contribute substantially to the content or methods of a practical theology. In relation to the church, this type is interested in the church as data to be studied, or simply as a matter of private interest. But Type IA takes little responsibility for the church's development. To the extent that practical theology focuses on the contributions of the social sciences to society in general, this type has a definite contribution to make.

Type IB. Practical theology can take the form of a critical science whose purpose is the formation of the church.

Here the primary interest is the formation and development of the identity and mission of the church, utilizing a critical scientific method. For example, the journal *Pastoral Psychology* was founded in 1950 with a special emphasis on psychological concerns, making a commitment to help ministers cope with persons seeking such help. The journal's purpose reflects the type of practical theology labeled IB, bringing the best re-sources of secular interest to bear on the ultimate good of the church. The editors reasoned that if people in the church are suffering because of a changing society, then the church is obligated to find the most effective means to help them.

The decision to publish our new Journal grew out of an awareness of a deeply felt need on the part of the minister for the insights and skills of dynamic psychology and psychiatry, presented in a way that has immediate and practical application to the minister's work, and within the religious framework of the pastor's point of view.[4]

The concern here is to help the church and its leadership, and the focus is on scientific theory and skills as a source of insight and training. The strength of this type of practical theology is the sincere desire to bring the best quality of care to persons who are suffering and the willingness to use whatever strategies are available in order to accomplish this. This type is based on a theology of openness to the wisdom of society and the courage to appropriate this wisdom even when it seems to challenge the traditional understanding of the church about its task and identity.

Included in this type are specialists in the church whose practical theology is based on a satellite science: pastoral counselors, educators, organizers, musicians, executives, missiologists, fund raisers, church growth specialists, social change experts, small group trainers, editors, and many others. In these specialists there is often a deep commitment to the church and its mission combined with a set of theories and skills based on a critical science. As the social sciences have become powerful influences in the larger culture, the leaders of the church have increasingly appropriated these insights for the use in the church.

Some of James Lapsley's insights favor such a definition of practical theology, although he is critical of the unreflective use of such methods and the tendency to avoid integration with theology. According to Lapsley, the primary focus of pastoral care is "guiding and improving the care of persons."[5] The pastor guides and cares for persons within the framework of a normative vision and a theological perspective. But Lapsley fears that an overemphasis on abstract forms of theology results in the loss of the central point of ministry, which is "the discernment of and appropriate strategies and tactics for attaining the *possibilities* of a particular person or persons."[6] This central concern is basic for those specialists who turn to the scientific disciplines for the major content of practical theology. It is the pressing need of persons for effective and competent pastoral action that leads this type of practical theology to obtain its norms and strategies from the satellite science that provides the best help and to use these insights for the benefit of the church.

The weakness of this type of practical theology is the possibility that the professional might lose touch with the Christian tradition. The difficulty comes at the limits of the scientific discipline. As the fields of psychology and psychotherapy become increasingly pluralistic and relative, it is easier for the professional to be oriented more around vocation and less around one's original religious tradition. A deeper theological orientation could provide a perspective from which to criticize shifting secular norms and strategies. However, if one has become separated from the tradition, reorientation back to the religious tradition is most difficult.

Donald Earl Miller's (not to be confused with one of the present writers) *The Case for Liberal Christianity* (Harper & Row, 1981) is an interesting example of using a social-scientific analysis (Durkheim, Freud, and others) to show the impotence of current secular social practices. He finds power for social solidarity in the church, but otherwise he finds historical affirmations of the church to be meaningless. His is a call to return to the church as a source of renewal for the society. While Miller's analysis may seem to be an analysis of the church for the sake of its mission, his "new case" turns out to be analysis of the formation of the larger society (Type IA).

Robert Bellah's writings also show the social functions of religion, but he finds an irreducible function of faith in religion. In that way, he is in the tradition of Ernst Troeltsch and Max Weber, whose analyses depend on a "religious a priori." One need not defend the conception of a religious a priori to see that they resisted the reduction of the church and its mission to social and economic forces. Their work is about the larger formation of society, but that in turn requires analysis of the church and its mission. Indeed, Troeltsch's work is so complex and subtle that, although he claimed to be applying a sociological method, he was also in dialogue with the Christian theological tradition (Type IIA).

In terms of its relation to philosophy and science Type IB finds its primary identity in a particular philosophy or science and its positions are often indistinguishable from those of scholars and practitioners in the field. In terms of its relation to the Christian story and tradition, this type uses the tradition in several ways. For some, the Christian story provides certain abstract norms for its generally utilitarian ethic, such as neighbor love, individual worth, or growth. However, it is the scientific identity and not the religion that provides the content of these norms. The tradition is sometimes used to justify the particular form of science that is one's identity, such as "behaviorism is more Christian than humanistic psychology," or "socialism is more Christian than capitalism." Yet, another option exists. The tradition can provide content for theological reflection on the human experience after the scientific framework has been established. A systematic theologian can be invited to a case conference for dialogue, or an ethicist to a meeting of social action reformers. Under such circumstances, traditional terminology may be already established by science and so the tradition is often not helpful, revealing, or practical.

In the face of those options, the relation of this type of practical theology to the church is best understood in terms of interest and commitment. While theory and methods come from science, such specialties are based

41

in the church. The church provides the setting in which practical theology is utilized and the insights from science are applied for the benefit of the church and its mission to society.

What makes this method theological is the commitment to a vision of person, society, or history that is implicit within the social scientific or philosophical concepts being employed. If an analysis of benefit is being made and acted upon within a church, then an implicit utilitarianism is at work. To the extent that a utilitarian conception of society is acted upon, that utilitarian view takes on at least a quasi-religious function. We agree with Paul Tillich that such quasi-religious concepts can function as theology even when they are not explicitly in touch with the Christian tradition. In fact, much social scientific analysis in the church does function as theology. To speak of quasi-theology does not mean that practical theology can get along quite nicely without the secular scientific disciplines. Traditional theology itself has come under the criticism of scientific disciplines, so that criticism is a two-way street. Therefore, even though the scientific axis is only on the edge of being theology proper, its relation to theology is so significant and its function so theological that it must be included in a typology of practical theology. When the quasi-religious conceptions of person, society, or history are examined in relation to the Christian tradition, then the characteristics of Type II appear.

Type IIA. Practical theology can take the form of a critical correlation of the Christian tradition and contemporary philosophy and science in its concern for the formation of society.

In this context the church is important as a subsystem of society in which faith is created and nurtured, but practical theology must be a philosophical discipline concerned with public ethics. Browning argues for the public character of practical theology.

[The Hiltner-Williams correlational method] certainly started with faith, but it brought the intuitions of faith into the public arena, fostered public discussion, reflected critically on the facts of faith, and attempted to advance publicly defensible reasons for the relevance of faith within the context of the public hospital, the public healing disciplines, and other public communities that are the context for our common lives.[7]

The assertion of the public character of practical theology means that the discipline so understood is essentially philosophical, even though it begins with Christian faith. "Pastoral Theology should be understood as philosophical reflection on the major themes of the Judeo-Christian tradition with special regard for the implication of these themes for a normative vision of the human life cycle."[8] In this emphasis on the character of practical theology as philosophical and public, Browning agrees with Tracy.

My aim is to suggest one basic heuristic schema for practical theology as public theology. My claim is that practical theology attains its public character by articulating praxis criteria of human transformation as well as an explicitly theological ethic.[9]

Thus it is evident that, while starting with Christian faith and theological themes from the Judeo-Christian tradition, the basic thrust of Type IIA is toward a critical correlation that informs the development of society.

The method of this practical theology is "critical correlation." One form of this method involves several steps: a phenomenological description of contemporary human experience, a restatement of Christian themes in contemporary and public language and symbols, an examination of the contemporary sciences for their descriptive and normative statements about human life, and a philosophical correlation of these sources.[10]

[The revised correlational method] aspires to correlate an historically and hermeneutically accurate interpretation of the Christian fact, the life and ministry of Jesus Christ, with a philosophically understandable and publicly verifiable interpretation of the structures of common human experience.[11]

"I hope to define the practical theology of care in such a way as to give it both respectability within the disciplines of theology as well as plausibility among the disciplines pursued in the universities of our land."[12] The reference to the universities gives a clue about the setting in which this type of practical theology is most attractive. Christian scholars and theologians who have a deep conviction that the Christian tradition has important truths which should be a part of the public discussion of norms, and who are committed to a modern apology of the Christian faith, are attracted to the critical correlation type of practical theology. In order to gain credibility among scholars of other disciplines, the particular and idiosyncratic confessional claims of the various traditions must be restated in universal and philosophical language and symbols. Otherwise, the claims of the denomination, or even of the ecumenical church, are dismissed as being limited to particularized communities, and are not relevant to the establishment of a public ethic that will unite a society in the midst of competing claims. This type of practical theology recognizes that modern pluralism in a democratic society cannot allow domination by an interest group with a narrow tradition. Every interest group must compete for recognition in the public arena in order to be influential.

Advocates of a critical correlation method of practical theology accept the validity and reality of this type of society. They believe that the Christian tradition does have a contribution to make to the public debate about norms for human life, but that the church has no special right to a hearing in the public meeting. The church must universalize its symbols and earn its right to participation in the public debate just as does any other interest group. The task of theologians is to move from the insights of the church and its tradition into the larger society in order to enrich and transform society. A church that refuses to move this way deserves to be irrelevant and ignored. The future of society may depend on persons who are the product of the Christian tradition becoming involved and committed to the public discussion in a pluralistic setting.

Critical correlation points to the fact of an essentially equal dialogue between theology and science. Tracy calls this "a collaborative exercise."

In sum, these first three collaborative steps for practical theology will be involved in disciplined reflection upon the possible mutually critical correlations obtaining between secular models of moral praxis with an emancipatory thrust and Christian faith praxis.[13]

Even though one starts with the insights of tradition, these insights have no logical priority within the dialogue itself. The claims from the tradition must demonstrate their validity alongside all other claims according to public criteria. Within this dialogue, science may contribute constructively to the development of theological norms, and theology may criticize the normative horizon of scientific theory. Ultimately, both theology and science are enriched by the debate.[14]

In terms of the relation of practical theology to the Christian tradition, the tradition provides the starting intuitions.

> The revised correlational method in practical theology that the three of us [Browning, Tracy, McCann] propose goes beyond the simple desire to center practical theology on the church's presence in the world. It wants this presence to both start in faith yet end in a mutually critical diaogue between Christianity and other perspectives toward the end of shaping a common life.[15]

These intuitions from the tradition are a continuing influence on the direction of practical theology, but they must be translated into public symbols, thereby establishing dialogue with other perspectives.

In terms of the relation of practical theology to the church, Type IIA acknowledges the church as the preserver of the tradition and as a source of the scholars who are committed to bringing the insights of the tradition into the public arena. However, this type is concerned that the Christian fact may be limited to a particular concrete community in outdated and inaccessible language and that its symbols will, therefore, not contribute to the transformation and enrichment of the larger society. The church can be an important source of insight into the human condition if it is willing to risk its claims in the public arena. But the church may remain irrelevant to the public discussion, and therefore be irresponsible in its role as a creative subsystem of society. To the extent that practical theology is concerned with the correlation of insights from many sources with the development of a public ethic, this is a valid type.

Type IIB. Practical theology can take the form of a critical correlation in terms of method which focuses primarily on the formation of the church as a community of faith.

The definition of practical theology by Fowler is an example of Type IIB. Fowler's method involves the correlation of insights from the tradition with theories of development and virtue from the human sciences. Yet he locates practical theology within a concrete community of faith. Fowler reveals the nature of his method when he notes, "practical theology carries on critical conversation with the social sciences, the arts, and literature."[16] Fowler's method is very much like Tracy's "mutual critical correlation," in which theologians engage in dialogue with scientists on an equal footing based on criteria acceptable to both.

At the same time, Fowler defines practical theology as

theological reflection and construction arising out of and giving guidance to a community of faith in the praxis of its mission. Practical theology is critical and constructive reflection on the praxis of the Christian community's life and work in its various dimensions.[17]

Fowler affirms Schleiermacher's position when he says that practical theology joins an "ecclesial interest and a scientific spirit."[18]

Ogletree describes practical theology in similar terms. In his construction of the content of practical theology, he employs terms that are neither strictly religious nor theological. For Ogletree the essence of practical theology involves three dimensions of human life: the meaning dimension, the action dimension, and the self-in-community dimension.[19] This language is from existential philosophy and could easily be a part of the university dialogue. Yet, Ogletree is interested in the formation of the church as a concrete community. Practical theology "concerns our ways of enacting Christian faith in the building up of the church and in the implementation of its mission to the world."[20] It is at this point that Browning is critical of Ogletree in a way that identifies the differences between Type IIA and Type IIB.

Ogletree, on the other hand, although building a place for theory as a distancing moment within the life of praxis, seems primarily interested in theory for what it can do to teach the faithful and less interested in a revised correlational dialogue with other praxis models in our pluralistic situation.[21]

This type values philosophical methods and collaboration across disciplinary lines between theology and the sciences, but locates practical theology primarily within the activity of the church as a concrete community. On the one hand, Type IIB understands theology as only one perspective among many within a pluralistic society which must argue for its methods and right to be heard alongside other perspectives. Therefore, it is a public and philosophical discipline that brings its findings to the public arena and claims no priority to revelation within this setting. On the other hand, this type emphasizes the crucial importance of a concrete Christian community for the survival of theology itself.

Accordingly, this type perceives that theology, as a discipline, an academic exercise, does not spring directly out of the Christian tradition and does not represent only a perspective alongside other disciplines in modern society. Rather, theology is deeply dependent on a concrete community of believers who try to be faithful in the modern world. Theology does not exist mainly as a discipline, but arises out of the need of Christian communities to define their identity in ways that make sense in the world. Therefore, practical theology is a discipline "arising out of and giving guidance to a community of faith."[22] Without a concrete community there is no need for a practical theology because its philosophical and public task is not sufficient to sustain it. But when a concrete community tries to be articulate about its own nature and experience, it must adopt publicly accessible language and symbols. Fowler supports Browning's description of the critical correlation method:

I am grateful for Browning's leadership toward the recovery of normative foundations in pastoral care. I am glad he integrally relates his way of formulating normative principles both to Jewish and Christian roots, and to theories of the life cycle. I share with him the conviction that our expressions of moral concern and efforts at ethical guidance must be publicly intelligible and rationally explicated, and when necessary, rationally defended. . . . I do not wish to ignore either the concerns about pluralism and significance of a public language and rational foundation for accounting for the convictions, goals, and methods of Christian nurture.[23]

But Fowler's reasons for his interest in the community of faith stress the rich traditional and archetypal aspects of theology.

Two factors, however, lead me to stress more the ecclesial character of practical theology. . . .

First, *formation* in faith may and should prepare one for fruitful contributions to a pluralistic society. But if effective, formation in faith means formation in relation to the centers of value, the images of power, the rituals and normative stories *of a particular community*. . . .

Second, our commitment to honoring pluralism may mean biting our tongue when, by heritage and vocation, we have access to something in the richness of Christian faith and the power of God that can *really* help. . . . In our concern for

49

public language and for rational foundations for our theologies let us not underestimate the archetypal and historical power of the cross and resurrection, the universal longing for messiah, and the deep rationality of our response, in kind, to a universal love.[24]

Both Browning and Fowler are interested in the transformative character of faith in society. However, Browning insists that its public and transformative character remain foremost. Fowler suggests that the public transformative character may not always be evident. Historically, transformation has had its roots in times of exile, crucifixion, and persecution, times in which the community somehow endured in spite of what appeared to be the loss of effectiveness. If IIA is clearly transformational, IIB has a paradoxical relation to transformation.

In summary, this type of practical theology combines a critical correlation method with a primary interest in the concrete church as a community of faith. It is a perspective willing to engage the sciences in a mutual collaboration, and to bring the insights of the Christian tradition to the public arena in terms of language and symbols. Because this type strongly believes that the passion of theology depends on having its roots deep within a particular community, it is skeptical of the ability of theology to sustain itself as solely a philosophical discipline. To the extent that practical theology is concerned with correlating insights from the various disciplines for the formation of the vitality and adventure of the concrete church, this type is valid.

Type IIIA. Practical theology can take the form of critical confession with a primary emphasis upon the church's vision for the larger society.

"Confession" refers to a method which focuses primarily on interpretation and reinterpretation of the Christian story and tradition and treats this story as normative for today. The Christian story is not normative in an uncritical way. Rather, the critical confessional method is self-critical and willing to examine its cognitive assumptions and its social location. It seeks to discover the truth about the tradition so that Christians today can find interpretations of their experience which are congruent with the history of God's revelation.[25] This method tends to be suspicious of and cautious about the role of philosophy and science, while at the same time it takes the dialogue with these forms of wisdom seriously. But there is a suspicion that alien norms will usurp the center of any system that is based on mutual collaboration with science. The most important aspect of this type is a sustained effort to understand the depth of the Christian tradition so that modern faith will be continuous with the Christian story rather than continuous with the modern world.

Leander Keck argues for a practical theology of preaching which features confession as its central dynamic.

In the last analysis, we too cannot rest a theology of preaching from the canon only on a phenomenological understanding of texts in communities, but we must grapple with the question of how such a canon is related to God. At this point we shift to another mode of discourse, that of doxology and confession, for to speak of the canon as the vehicle of God's word is to confess that through this text as through none other we have heard a word, experienced reality, in such a compelling way that the Ground of being and value has made itself known.[26]

Confession is the heart of practical theology of this type, while scientific methods play a secondary role.

Another form of this method is described in *The*

Politics of Jesus by John Howard Yoder. He states at the beginning of this book that his goal is to provide an interpretation of the New Testament view of Jesus in the Gospel of Luke so that it will be normative for social ethics today. He criticizes modern theological ethics for its ignorance of the empirical Jesus, and its use of abstract definitions of Christ as a cover for a philosophical ethic that is more consistent with modern society than with the biblical Christ.

When, for instance, Jesus is spoken of as "unveiling true humanity," or when incarnation is spoken of as revelation, this could well mean that we could or should go to the man Jesus in all his contingent humanity to see what kind of man God wants. Yet in the actual practice of contemporary "incarnational theology" this language generally serves as the preamble to or as validation for a definition of essential or common humanity derived from quite other sources, which incarnation is held to have ratified.[27]

Here Yoder seems to be criticizing a method of correlation which brings the biblical tradition into essentially equal dialogue with secular interpretations. He suspects that this method usually results in the Christian tradition being taken less seriously than the modern norms dominating the discussion. Yoder wants, instead, to start with the assumption that the texts about Jesus are normative for Christians and should be normative in any discussion about the form and content of modern theology.

In both Type IIIA and Type IIIB, there tends to be agreement about the definition of theology and its relation to the church. "Theology is that activity (or product of the activity) of any historical religious community in which it attempts to ascertain its own nature, reality, and truth." Mudge defines practical theology as "the discipline which enables the church to become critically aware of the sense it makes by what it is, does, and says." By the "church" he means "the community of faith in its social and cultural context."[28]

Thus, practical theology is an activity of the church as it articulates its identity in the modern society. According to Graydon Snyder, "Theology for the Free Church means primarily the faith reflection of the community in light of God's will and the socio-political world in which it lives."[29] Thomas Groome defines practical theology in terms of "shared praxis": "Christian religious education by shared praxis can be described as a group of Christians sharing in dialogue their critical reflection on present action in light of the Christian story and its vision toward the end of lived Christian faith."[30]

The above commentaries agree in defining theology as an activity of the church in determining its identity within the world. This definition of theology with reference to the church is partly a result of the confessional method which turns to the Christian tradition as normative and is cautious about the influence of philosophy and science.

The prevailing doctrine of the church distinguishes Type IIIA from Type IIIB. Is the concrete church to be judged in its life and witness primarily by a faith-informed vision of what is possible for the total society (IIIA), or is the empirical embodiment of the Christian story within the community of faith to be the final judge of all other conceptions brought to it (IIIB)?

Throughout Christian history much practical theology has been measured against what is conceived to be actually possible for the total society. Luther believed that the church had to compromise its concrete commitment to Christ in order to survive in the world. Therefore, while the church holds to a Christian vision, it must also be guided by what is necessary in the world at large. At best, the kingdom of God can be approximated in relationships within the family and possibly certain other interpersonal relationships. The kingdom of the world is governed by certain created orders. The church lives within both kingdoms at one and the same time. Christians are called to live according to the kingdom of God, but given the forgiveness and grace to live in the kingdom of the world. Christians are to live so that love will transform the orders of the world whenever possible, whenever God so ordains. The Christian ethic is therefore very much shaped by what is possible in the total society.[31]

Calvin developed a systematic theology according to which the church is the key to the organization of all society.[32] On the one hand the congregation is to be faithful to the covenant with God, and on the other hand the covenant that governs the congregation is destined to be the pattern that governs all society. The concern for a pattern that is appropriate for all society is characteristic of Type IIIA. The power of the Calvinist tradition is that it has an ecclesial vision of the total society. Troeltsch referred to this as the sectarian vision enlarged to include the whole of society. However, Calvin attempts to derive practical theological conclusions from the central affirmations of faith. Calvin's argument that lending institutions may charge interest is instructive. Since land may be rented with part of the harvest returned to the landowner as rent, so may money also be loaned with part of the renter's profit returned to the lender. Since God has clearly allowed the one, God will allow the other. Here one can see a theological analysis for the behavior of the believer working as a model for the total society. This particular argument revolutionized the Western world.

The Roman Church has also held to an ideal of the church as a source of moral guidance for all of society.

That role was more nearly approximated in medieval society than at any other time in history. Those in the religious orders are called to special vows that approximate the gospel requirements most clearly. Everyone else is called to live according to the necessities and circumstances of their own situations. The moral law, therefore, is intended to give some moral guidance to the formation of the total society.[33]

Each of the historical positions just mentioned is characterized by a compromise of a faith perspective for the sake of what is possible in the total society. Troeltsch in *The Social Teaching of the Christian Churches* develops in exquisite detail this theme of the church living according to a confessional pattern which time and again must be compromised according to the circumstances and requirements of the total society. Therefore, the church sees its vision as a primary source of moral guidance for society.

A contemporary expression of the church's confessional vision for all of society is to be found in Edward Farley's conception of "ecclesial presence."

There is, it seems, a region, an inclusive reality to which theological understanding and theological science are correlated. . . . I would submit that ecclesiality or ecclesial existence is that region. I mean by that something partly given in history and something ideal, normative, and eschatological. . . . Perhaps the central and perennial problem of grasping ecclesial presence lies here, how can it be redemptively pervasive of any and all social, political, and cultural spaces, without itself becoming identical with any of them and developing official, timeless, ecclesial-political institutions.[34]

Farley seeks a definition of church which can be used to identify the faithfulness of the church in relation to the Christian tradition's capacity to redeem any and all

55

social, political, and cultural spaces without losing itself totally in them.

Mudge seems to move closer to confessional faithfulness as the center of the church, but still he is guided by a conception of the total society. He seeks to develop a critical ecclesiology by which the church can be organized. Wanting to give greater consideration to the empirical church, Mudge has defined his interest as discovering how the social reality of the church actually works, as opposed to how it ought to work according to some larger social ideal. "How can we understand the thinking that must go on in the process by which the church comes into being and remains in being? What would it mean to think theoretically about the way the church must think operationally?"[35] Along with Ricoeur, Mudge examines the patterns of behavior which make up all society reality. "The many possible actions in a social repertoire arrange themselves into repeated, statistically commonplace, interrelated patterns which in turn make up the typified texture of the society as a whole."[36]

In these patterns as texts, reality is seen to be ambiguous. He suspects that much of what occurs in the empirical church is incoherent, and so believes it imperative that the church develop a model of thinking that can guide it. Seeking the "true center" of the church, Mudge notes, "The church is the world as it is meant to be in Jesus Christ, the space where the world is structured according to its true center."[37] These statements formulate the boundary between the last two described types. Type IIIA holds the tradition as normative and the church as the locus of practical theology. But finally it holds to a faith-informed vision of what is possible for the total society against which any particular expression of church life can be judged.

This type looks first to the possibilities and circumstances of the larger community rather than the processes of the faith community. The total community's sense of reason takes on high importance. To the extent that practical theology is a search to let the total society be informed by the Christian tradition, this is a valid type.

Type IIIB. Practical theology can take the form of critical confession that is centered in the practice of a concrete community of Christian faith in mission.

The theological tradition is normative in relation to philosophy and science. The church must continually work with a careful hermeneutic to interpret and reinterpret the Christian story. This type reflects an increasing interest in the community of faith as the interpreter of truth.

The concrete social reality of the church becomes the locus of authority for normative theology in several ways. Part of the discussion revolves around the relative authority of the ordained ministry and the local church. David Steinmetz identifies an ambiguity in Luther that leaves open the discussion of whether the pastor or the community of faith is the source of authority.

The Congregationalists resolved Luther's dilemma by emphasizing the priority of the congregation. For Congregationalists, as for Presbyterians, the pastor is a bishop or teaching elder. However, unlike the Catholics who argue no bishop, no Church, the Congregationalists argue no Church, no bishop. The Church exists as a covenant community before a pastor is called.[38]

On the issue of authority in the church, John Cobb suggests that the traditional authorities in theology have collapsed with our awareness of the pluralism in these authorities themselves. These include Scripture, tradition, and reason. He notes that what remains after the

57

collapse of these authorities is the community of faith as it struggles to discern the truth for its time. It is the development of community consensus that allows the church community to act with conviction on critical issues.[39] Seeking a consensus within the community of faith on the critical issues facing its life within the modern world is a kind of practical theology.

Such a view echoes Graydon Snyder's response to Farley. Snyder describes Farley's view as one of correspondence truth, in which concrete life in community must "correspond" to some revealed truth. The absence of traditional authority makes this view problematic because there is no agreement about revealed truth. Snyder suggests that an alternative is a consensus view of truth. By this he means that truth is known through the process of the community together "seeking the 'mind of Christ' in light of Scripture."[40] There is no objective truth to which the community of faith can order its life. Rather, truth is revealed as the community struggles to order its life together, and theology is the reflection that emerges when the church engages in this process to reach consensus.

Troeltsch reaches for such a view in his *Social Teaching of the Christian Churches*. There, he argues that a new evaluative vision for the church must come from the story of the church's ongoing vision. This must be an empirical study and must be subject to social criticism. He was searching for a new universal social vision for Christianity. The fact that his great study did not produce such a vision has been considered by some to be his failure. However, one can also understand Troeltsch to have uncovered the radical pluralism within which the modern world lives. We have the actual empirically embodied vision of the Christian story leading always to an evaluational stance in society at large, but such a vision is never adequate as a formal model for the total society. Rather, the ongoing search for a consensus continues as the various communities of faith dialogue for a more adequate living embodiment of their own faith. In Type IIIB the ideal community of faith constantly moves through the ongoing living praxis of the community.

If Type IIIA has confidence that the visions of life in the Scriptures will transform society, Type IIIB believes that the relationship of church and the larger society is more complex. Local Christian communities are called faithfully to express the historical confession in their shared life whether or not the transformation of society is immediately evident. In some historical periods, church communities and the larger society will be engaged in meaningful dialogue and some transformation of each will result. In other historical periods, the practice of local communities of faith will be ignored, trivialized, or even persecuted. While the transformation of society is the hope and mission of the church for Type IIIB, the center of community life is faithfulness to the confession in actual practice. This means that theology itself is subject to testing for its meaning and truth in the shared life of empirical communities of faith.

In summary, this type of practical theology uses a critical confessional method that values the Christian story and tradition over philosophy and science. The unique aspect of this type is the commitment to the shared practice of concrete communities of faith and the willingness to allow these empirical communities to judge the interpretation of the tradition and to correlate its theology with other interpretations of human life. The collapse of traditional authorities and a renewed interest in the sociology of Christian life indicated strong interest in such a practical theology, one that focuses on the practice of faith in the world rather than in theory only. But is this not scandalous? How can particular, ambiguous, finite, and fallible community be the source of truth about knowledge of God and love of Christ? To such a query, the "consensus" view replies that community is all we have: shared life is not finally rational and unambiguous, but it is the locus of God's activity. For a tradition that has continually searched for the clarity of ideals, the possibility of such a theology is most troublesome. To the extent that practical theology is a search for new ways to interpret and live the Christian tradition within the concrete community of faith in its mission to the world, this is a valid type.

Summary and Conclusions

This chapter identifies two axes around which the questions in practical theology can be organized, and these two axes yield six ideal types or models of practical theology. There are three types of method: critical science, critical correlation, and critical confession. There are two types of description of the church-society relationship, one tending toward interest in the formation of society and the development of universal norms and strategies for the social order, and one tending toward interest in the formation of the church and its faithful action in the world.

This typology suggests several questions for our consideration.

1. What is the critical method that is followed in a model of practical theology? Does it tend to value tradition over science, science over tradition, or seek a mutual correlation between them? How are social, psychological, political, economic, and existential tendencies to distortion and ideology uncovered? In what context would such a method be most helpful and what are its limitations?

2. What is the locus of interest, formation of society

or formation of the church? Is the product of practical theology intended to be public and universal, benefiting society, or is it intended for the benefit of a particular concrete community in its mission to society? What are the values and limitations of this form of practical theology?

What must be our vision for such discussions of practical theology? Obviously, there are multiple ways in which practical can be defined. A strong case can be made for any one of the types we have identified. Undoubtedly, these various types of practical theology will continue, as they have in the past. In our view, they tend to enrich one another. We believe that the confessional can never be reduced to the scientific or philosophical. Conversely, the confessional becomes arid and uninformed without the scientific and philosophical awareness. We also believe that truth moves through concrete praxis, and therefore we favor the community of faith reaching out in mission. However, our position as seminary teachers may unduly influence us. Those in other settings will surely be influenced toward another type. Practical theology is formed and reformed in an open dialogue between all the types. Even while favoring a dialogical confessional community stance, we urge the ongoing discussion among the various types we have identified.

T H R E E

A Method for Practical Theology

Practical theology is critical and construc-tive reflection within a living community about human experience and interaction, involving a correlation of the Christian story and other perspectives, leading to an interpretation of meaning and value, and resulting in everyday guidelines and skills for the formation of persons and communities.

The complexity of this definition is necessary because we are trying to account for the important steps in a credible method of practical theology. Later we will demonstrate more simple forms of this method when we suggest six steps by which this process can be followed by a lay committee in a local congregation.

We borrowed the term "critical and constructive reflection" from James Fowler[1] because it combines several elements that need to be held together. For any theology to be credible today, it must be critical in the sense used by David Tracy and others.[2] "Critical" means more than awareness of the analytical methods of socio-historical research, although it includes this. "Critical" also means continuous self-criticism to become aware of the biases, assumptions, and self-inter-ests that continually influence one's perceptions. Criticism includes a method of exploring conceptual bias that results from socio-economic, political, and psychological forces. Such critique must permeate any theological method or else it remains naive and liable to be narrowly self-serving. Such critique must be featured in our method.

But practical theology must be more than analytical; it must also be constructive and evaluative. Theology must include constructive affirmations and assessments about meaning and value in human events. Such a constructive assessment includes both descriptive and normative elements. It gives a perspective both on what is and what ought to be. The description of what is or what is true occurs from the disinterested position of the observer, while an assessment of value occurs from interest of one who is engaged and (potentially) active in the account.

One can always give a disinterested cognitive interpretation of the meaning of an event. The method of practical theology, as we are proposing it, requires a discernment of value in the interpretation of an event. In fact, every interpretation already has an evaluative element. To move further and make the evaluative perspective explicit is essential for practical theology. The discernment of value includes not only the continuity of the event, but such things as the priorities, obligations, responsibilities, misconceptions, weaknesses, tendencies, larger purposes, as well as God's will and purposes. A move to the guidelines for practice always stands within a narrative discernment of causes, values, possibilities, and purposes. Some weaker or stronger intentionality is implicit in every narrative account of a human event. The discernment of value requires making explicit the intentional character of the narrative.[3]

Practical theology is reflection, which means that it is not the same as lived experience. Practical theology is a form of disciplined thought about experience which is an abstraction from community interaction. Thus, it is not whatever a community does in its life together. Rather, it is a form of thinking about life. Its purpose is to clarify perceptions about the structures and tendencies of experience, but it is always less than full experience and must be tested within experience frequently to verify and correct its claims.

"Within a living community" points to the communal nature of all theology. Scholars are appointed by communities to work diligently and carefully on their behalf. But finally, theology is an activity of a living community as it tries to discern the truth and meaning of its life in the modern world. Academic theolgy is dependent on the specific concrete community to which it is responsible. This turns the question of authority on its head. The task of practical theology is not to discover the clear and distinct ideas of truth to which communities must conform their lives. Rather, the task of practical theology is to discover more adequate ways of articulating the depth, richness, and possibilities of life as they are found in concrete communities. We are interested in pursuing the idea of the community collectively engaged in theological reflection, and particular scholars as the community's servants.

"Human experience and interaction" identifies the empirical principle that underlies this method, about which we will speak later. For now, we can say that the underlying momentum of the practical theology discussion comes from our need to find more adequate ways to speak about the richness of experience. Theology has a history of being primarily cognitive. The discovery of the radical socio-historical nature of experience is forcing theology to reevaluate its basic assumptions.[4] This process of reevaluation can lead to a renewal of practical theology. One way to conceive of this issue is to say that theology must begin and end in the richness of historical-lived experience and interaction, and cannot be rooted in another separated world of ideas or revelation.

The phrase "human experience and interaction" is intended to point out that experience is not to be interpreted only subjectively. Experience includes interaction, but conversely, interaction is always being experienced. The word "interaction" signifies that action always occurs within a network of responses and anticipated responses. Even the most isolated action is a response to acts of others that have already occurred and an anticipation of future acts of others. Therefore, even the most isolated act is an interaction.[5] The phrase "human experience and interaction," therefore, anticipates a community context.

Our concern for reflection about human experience and interaction is in touch with what some are calling "praxis." The term, praxis, often refers to the reflection of a community upon that interaction in which it is already engaged. The concern is that thought will not be separated from intentions, purposes, projects, and actions. Therefore, the term "praxis" has come to refer to the unity of purposeful activity and the thoughtful consideration of that activity. Praxis always involves engagement of the self, the network of decisions leading from the past into the present and the future. We share with those who feature the term "praxis" the concern that practical theology originate in human interaction so as to be intimately connected to future interaction.[6]

"Correlation of the Christian story and other perspectives" means that the sciences must be taken as serious dialogue partners and that correlation between a faith perspective and other perspectives is necessary for practical theology.

"Leading to an interpretation of meaning and value in

human life" points again to the move from descriptive and analytical thought to normative statements. The discontinuity of "is" and "ought" is bridged by the risk of confession, and it is a joint risk of will and imagination that must be taken for truth to be known.

"Resulting in everyday guidelines and skills" means that practical theology cannot remain only an abstract cognitive endeavor. Practical theology must start with a deep awareness of the richness of concrete experience, and it must return to experience with well-developed practical metaphors, guidelines, and responsibilities for life in community. This, however, is more than applied theology, because the practical implications of theology provide a test of the validity of its interpretation. If a particular interpretation cannot be translated into constructs and plans that actually shape community life, then validity of the interpretation is called into question. Furthermore, particular situations often require the reconceptualization of central theological ideas. This dialogical movement between concrete experience and abstract thinking is essential to the method of practical theology.

"Formation of persons and communities" points to our understanding of the goal of practical theology and, indeed, of reflection itself. The direction of God's activity in history is toward individuals and communities of greater quality. By this we mean the emergence of persons and communities who can integrate greater complexity and alienation into their being without losing integrity. The achievement of such persons and communities is beauty according to Whitehead, theonomy according to Tillich, and the kingdom of God in the Bible.

Empirical Method in Theology

Before we continue with a description of the essential components of our method, we want to say a

word about the empirical and phenomenological theologies that undergird its development. We have been
influenced both by American empirical process theology
as well as by continental phenomenological theology.
Our method has roots in both traditions.

American empirical theology is based on the assumption that experience provides the source and authority
for all reflection, including theology. For Daniel Day
Williams, this assumption has four parts. First, "by
experience I mean the felt, bodily, psycho-social organic
action of human beings in history."[7] This means that
experience cannot be reduced to some part of experience, such as sense perception, conscious experience,
cognitive experience, intuition and feeling, religious
experience, or any other kind. Rather, there is a
thickness and depth to experience which is more than
our attempts to describe and clarify it. It is this thicker
experience which is both social and historical, and which
is the reason for all reflection and the test of its validity.

Second, God is, in some sense, a part of concrete
experience even though God is also transcendent.
Theology can be empirical because God's activity has a
particular referent within experience. It is this immanence which enables us to speak about God at all and
which makes our statements about a relationship with
God intelligible. Empirical theology is involved in
articulating the conditions for God's involvement in
immediacy.

Third, the possibility of meaning and evaluation in
human life requires some process of reflection or
abstraction. Without reflection, humans would be
subject to being overwhelmed and confused by the
buzzing reality of concrete data which would allow no
conscious freedom. There are ways of reflecting on
concrete experience which can increase our freedom to
shape life toward greater value. Thus, life is a constant

67

dialectic of immersion in experience and distancing from it in order to clarify choices. Theology is a form of disciplined reflection upon experience designed to sensitize us to the activity of God so we can harmonize our decisions with God's actions and purposes.

Fourth, the danger of the reflective process is the impoverishment of the richness of experience. Abstractions and generalizations always feature some structures over others, and while they clarify some things, they distort, trivialize, and hide others. Therefore, all abstractions, including theology, must be held tentatively and self-critically, and must continually be tested against experience in its depth. There is always the sterile and dangerous tendency of reducing experience to one dimension. Experience continually teaches us about its truth and depth, and we must beware of living totally in an abstract world which tempts us with its clarity, but slays us with its shallowness.

Analogous tendencies can be found in the phenomenological tradition that comes through Dilthey, Troeltsch, and Husserl. Their intention was to get to the substratum of exprience, *Erlebniss,* as Dilthey called it. The phenomenological tradition attempts to explore the underlying unity of subject and object. It, therefore, finds all experience as perceived to be self-engaging, even in the perception. This suggests that attention to any description of experience must at the same time attend the character of intentionality both in what is being perceived and in the act of perception. Such considerations lead to the disclosure of the self-engagement of individuals, networks of individuals, and human communities. One may always return to the richness of the phenomena as perceived.

The phenomenological tradition also works at the particular referent of religious language. Whether Schleiermacher's feelings of absolute dependence,

Otto's sense of the Holy, or Tillich's ultimate concern, in every case one finds an effort to clarify the sense of religious language.

These assumptions drawn from empirical and phenomenological theologies guide our thinking about method in practical theology. The method begins and ends with experiences, and in between tries to be responsible to the levels of abstraction that are necessary to be rigorous, logical, and coherent.

The Essential Components of Practical Theology

Based on this definition of practical theology and the empirical principle, our method has the following components:

1. Description of lived experience
2. Critical awareness of perspectives and interests
3. Correlation of perspectives from culture and the Christian tradition
4. Interpretation of meaning and value
5. Critique of interpretation
6. Guidelines and specific plans for a particular community

Now one can begin to see the interplay of simplicity and complexity in this method. We suggest that these six steps are the essential components of practical theology from the most academic to the most pragmatic. In their simple form, these steps can be followed by a local church committee which is trying to research and plan a program for older persons in their community. They could begin by studying cases in a self-critical way, then look at the suggestions of gerontology research in dialogue with the Scriptures, make an interpretation of the meaning of their particular situation with awareness of their own self-interests, and then proceed to make detailed plans. In their complex form, a scholar, for example, could spend a lifetime trying to correlate the insights of feminism with the Bible. The complexity of the method will be demonstrated as we discover the difficulty of defining the nature of each of these steps and the methods appropriate to it. The rest of the chapter will focus primarily on this complexity and, based on this discussion, we can then proceed to describe the simpler forms.

The first step in practical theology is description of lived experience.

In order to understand the complexity of description, we have found Bernard Meland to be helpful. The logical and perceptual priority of all reflection is lived experience. When we become conscious we find ourselves in the middle of a "perceptual flux" which is the social and historical context for reflection. Thus, the first step of theology is attentiveness to this context in its thickness, including the structures of meaning already present there. Since lived experience is the context for reflection, and attentiveness is the proper stance toward it, we need to describe more carefully the nature of this lived experience and the character of attentiveness that is appropriate to it. When one attends to lived experience, whether it is a conversation with another person or an event such as the election of a president, one perceives a "complex of events, subtly and ambiguously envisaged" within a context of "relationships, where relationships are deemed experienceable." One is aware of the "thickness" of experience.[8]

Here one would be introduced to the threshold of a vital immediacy, the depth and mystery of which is such that one would be mindful that in attending it, one confronts holy ground. For in this immediacy of lived experience, all that has transpired as historic occurrence in the far reaches of space and time now transpires as concrete occurrence, merging in the distillations of history as lived with an emerging present, and carrying the import of both immediate and ultimate demands.[9]

In this paragraph, one picks up the main elements of experience, according to Meland. Present experience is a vital immediacy which is a configuration of relationships with all other beings. In addition, there is a "Creative Passage" at work within this immediacy that moves toward new structures of meaning in the future, and which has a sense of ultimacy about it. Thus, "immediacy and ultimacy traffic together."[10] Immediacy does not come into being as chaos, but it is already structured into meaning by the past and by its telos in the future. Attending to lived experience means opening oneself to this immediacy in its full depth, taking into oneself the meaning from the past in its ambiguous forms, and recognizing the presence of God with a telos for the future. This lived experience is a complex event that is inexhaustible in its depth and meaning, but not unstructured and chaotic.

Given this understanding of experience, including the immanence of God, what form can attentiveness take to be adequate to its richness and depth? Meland has coined the term "appreciative awareness"[11] to designate the attitude of openness to data that is involved in appropriate attending. The first part of attending is acknowledgment of the richness of experience and a willingness to expose oneself to an abundance of facts and relationships in order to let them have their influence in one's awareness.

In this act of reflection there is not simply a direct act of observation, but, as it were, a waiting and an expectancy that what is so envisaged will disclose its fuller pattern of meaning.[12]

It [this act] is holistic and appreciative, aiming at opening one's conscious awareness to the full impact of the concrete occurrence. It is very much like allowing one's visual powers to accommodate themselves to the enveloping darkness until, in their more receptive response to the shrouded shapes and forms concealed by the darkness, one begins to see into the darkness and to detect in it the subtleties of relationships and tendencies which had eluded one, but which now yield a visual field.[13]

After an active phase of collecting data which is adequate to one's purposes, there is an open and receptive phase, a listening phase, in which one allows the data to reveal their patterns and structures and avoids imposing meaning upon it.

But along with the openness of "appreciative awareness," there is an active discernment which restrains the tendency to see in experience the categories that one wants to see, and actively pursues the structures of meaning that are present in the events themselves. So attentiveness to lived experience depends on a rich definition of experience within its socio-historical context, an openness to experience as it presents itself, and a self-critical principle that guards against projections.

This method of practical theology begins with lived experience within its social and historical context of relationships. Immediate experience is internally related to the past in terms of causes and structures of meaning and to the future in terms of telos. Thus, lived experience has a depth and thickness that is inexhaustible. Attending to experience requires reflection in order to discover the internal meaning there rather than just the ambiguous flux of events that at first may appear chaotic. But reflection runs the danger of projecting abstractions onto experience which are sterile and inaccurate. Thus, theology must remain attentive to lived experience and continually return to empirical observation in order to test and revise its generalizations. God is active and immanent in lived experience, and the task of theology is to describe God's activity and purpose within this vital immediacy. Attentiveness to the depth of lived experience is a way of being attentive to the activity of God.

At this point, a question emerges, What is an adequate description? Given the empirical principle that assumes the richness and depth of lived experience, one answer is that every description is inadequate. As a pragmatic matter, we must assume that some descriptions are more adequate than others. However, there remains a variety of perspectives from which experience can be viewed, and one must be aware of the purpose for which any particular description is undertaken. The principle of self-critical awareness already is important in this first step. Description itself is already the interplay of experienced data and the perspective of the observer. As a matter of course, one must start where one is, but as a matter of method it is important for one to be aware of one's starting point. This dilemma of whether one begins with lived experience or with a self-critical awareness of one's perspective cannot easily be resolved and all the related issues are beyond the scope of this discussion. Our viewpoint is that one always begins in the middle with reality as perceived. This means that the awareness of lived experience is prior to the awareness of the relativity of one's perspective within experience. Therefore, one begins with a description of lived experience in whatever form it presents itself, and then proceeds to a form of criticism that leads to increased awareness of one's perspective. One strength of practical theology as a community process is that the description itself will lead to an awareness of the many ways in which description can be done. Lived experience calls for some description out of which a community becomes aware of its own diversity and the relativity of any one perspective. The task of practical theology is a process of building a community consensus about the structures of meaning in the life together.

One process of description has two interrelated steps. First, members of the community become aware of discrete events in the form of stories or conversations in which some discrepancy is involved. Something occurs which seems to challenge the way someone expects or hopes that things would happen. Second, when such events have enough interest or pain in them, the process of contextualization begins. The community dialogue looks for the broader web of relationships in which to place these events in order to understand them. Thus, the process of description involves the interplay of discrete events and contextualization. Both of these processes must be included in any description. The description of discrete events is important to keep the process rooted in data that are as concrete as possible. In counseling this may involve verbatim transcripts and audio or video tapes. In education this may involve verbatim transcripts or vignettes. In social action this may include descriptions of actions and conversations that are crucial to the story. The character of discrete events is that they are the most accessible parts of lived experience.

There are several problems with discrete events. One can always ask, Why these events and not those? For one reason or another an event is of interest to those who describe it. The interest, as we have said, may be due to some discrepancy, tension, or curiosity. The interest may be required by the larger context, longer purposes, or habitual concern. On the other hand, an interest may be due to resentment, anxiety, perversity, or some unacknowledged motive. A description can be either a way of engaging oneself or a means of hiding oneself. If the split between theory and practice is to be overcome, then the description of lived experience must move toward instances of self engagement, commitment, and risk. The concept of praxis presumes that the description of experience be a description of something in which one is already active and invested. Reflection upon such experience leads to the transformation of persons and communities. Nevertheless, there is a certain givenness to the selection of experience to be described. The question of selection finally drives a community to a confessional stance about its particular perspective.

Another problem with discrete events is that they are overdetermined.[14] This means that there is a variety of ways in which the relevant context can be described. For example, in any transcript of a conversation between two people, say between an Anglo female pastor and a Hispanic single father with two elementary school-age children, the relevant context is complex. We will list six possible contexts for such a conversation in order to make the point about overdetermination.

1. There is the context of personal history. Both of these persons have personal histories which partially determine their patterns of thinking, feeling, and behaving. It would be helpful to know these personal stories in order to understand the dynamics of the conversation.

2. There is the context of primary relationships. Both of these persons live within a network of intimate relationships—parents, children, friends—which determine much of who they are and what they are likely to do or not do.

3. There is the context of reference groups. The pastor and the father both have a larger network of reference groups which shape their identities—affilia-

tions with churches, professions, schools, clubs, and other groups. Such reference groups may be highly relevant to understanding any particular interaction: for example, being unemployed, being a member of a charismatic group, being a member of the National Rifle Association, being a part of a minority group. Such groups often define the expectations that people have of one another in specific events.

4. There is the context of culture. Both persons have their identities and expectations shaped by the particular culture they live in and the language they use. Sociologists and anthropologists have shown that culture is not just a way of expressing individual identity, but that culture and language largely define the perceptions and meanings that are possible for individual experience.

5. There is the context of gender. The feminists have shown that male and female experiences are often different. Some differences are the result of the subordination of women, and some are the result of different styles of development and socialization.

6. There is the context of majority/minority power. The political and socio-economic structures that define the relative power of persons in society also shape identity and expectations, and are relevant to context.

This partial list of the overlapping potentially relevant contexts for discrete events is intended to show the complexity of any description. Any of these contexts is potentially relevant and could receive inexhaustible attention. Lived experience is rich in depth because all experience occurs within a socio-historical context in which the relationships between events are important for context.

The first step of practical theology is a description of lived experience. On the one hand, this step involves attentiveness to lived experience wherever one is. It includes awareness of discrete events in the form of stories and conversations and the contextualization of these events in the form of the relationships that are relevant. However, even in this short summary we can see the complexity of description itself. The selection of discrete events already reveals the relativity of perspectives and the need for the observer to be aware of this relativity. The description of the relevant context is important for any understanding of discrete events, but the possible relevant context is beyond description. In addition, any description is already an abstraction from the depth of lived experience which may help clarify the structures of meaning there, but which will also distort and impoverish this depth of meaning. With full awareness of the complex issues of this step, we are suggesting that practical theology begins with a description of lived experience by a community that includes the hard data of discrete events and the crucial process of contextualization.

The second step of practial theology is critical awareness of perspective and interests.

Basic to every description is the network of relationships within which a description is carried out. Every description occurs within some community setting that is a unique perspective on the lived experience and in which are embedded both conscious and subconscious interests that influence perception. Description within a community will begin to reveal the relativity of various perspectives by uncovering diversity of perceptions. For example, if someone becomes concerned about inadequate nutrition for older persons in a community, someone else may be less concerned and may suggest that the extended families should meet that responsibility rather than the church. The difference in concern for this need will reveal differences in perspective, and this will challenge the community to test its commitment to pursuing this need. The second step is more than a precritical awareness of different opinions. Rather, this step requires a critical assessment of the perspectives and interests that are already embedded in the description, and a testing of whether the felt need that has been identified can become a focus of disciplined exploration by the total community.

A community that is self-critical about its perspective and interests therefore begins with a clarification of the underlying intentions, agreements, contracts, and covenants within the interacting group and an awareness of the interests and needs of other communities.[15] A description of a social event will be much different from that in a class, and that in turn will be much different from a business meeting or a therapy session. In each case the underlying contract or covenant is decisive for what is being described. The process of clarifying the contracts and interest may be done informally, as in a social event, or it may be done formally, as in a contract between a therapist and a client. Much of therapy depends on moving toward a working therapeutic covenant or alliance. All practical theology occurs within a covenant or other community relationship, and the clarification of the appropriate agreements is essential to practical theology.

Indeed, the tendency to be oblivious to, or to otherwise hide, the relational basis of perceptions leads to a series of systematic distortions. In therapy these distortions are spoken of as transference and counter-transference. The key to unearthing these distortions is a clarified relationship within a secure frame where the actual distortions can be interpreted. The therapeutic contract is an agreement to explore gradually the distortions that contaminate the open exploration of the common experience of therapy itself until there is transformation and healing.

Likewise, practical theology begins with the description of a felt need within a community, a shared praxis that seems incongruent with the lived experience of its members. This description is followed by a critical assessment of the covenants that inform and distort perceptions. The purpose of this assessment is to uncover, as much as possible, the perspectives and interests which lead to commitments and which also may unduly influence the continuing process of discovery.

This clarification of perspectives and interests also requires the awareness of the relationships, both direct and indirect, to other communities. The context for practical theology is the global community which includes many communities whose perspective and interests vary greatly from the local community where theological reflection occurs. Responsible practical theology always includes the perspectives and interests of other communities whose experience and future are affected by one's theologizing. The liberation theologians have made a clear case for the consideration of the world's poor as a part of the relevant context for the articulation of the meaning of the gospel in the modern world.

The result of a critical awareness of perspective and interest is the clarification of and recommitment to the basic covenants that hold the community together. This process may vary from a simple agreement in a class to discuss a certain topic of mutual interest, to a reconsideration of the goals and mission of the community, to a decision to reorganize a community to include new members with a different mission. In any case, practical theology involves a deliberate decision, informally or formally constituted, to join in a shared exploration of common experiences, practices, interests, issues, dilemmas. This shared exploration includes a commitment to pursue the truth wherever it may lead,

79

or in other language, to be open to the Spirit of God. The community is committing itself to a process of disciplined reflection on its shared life without full control over the results of that process. This commitment includes an openness to confess the interests that distort perceptions so that transformation is possible for the community and for the world to which it is in mission.

At times we have referred to this step of critical awareness of perception and interests as phenomenological analysis to emphasize the process of identifying the deeper themes of shared experience. Thematizing experience as a process begins to emerge as a community attends to description within the context of issues of covenant. Description involves self-critique at a fundamental level because every description reveals the relativity of perspectives.

On the one hand, reflection is a process that is causally related to experience. Finding meaning in experience requires reflection or else experience is just a buzzing chaos of discrete events. Whatever data are present in experience stimulate a process of generalization which is called for by the events themselves. The content of the reflective process will always have an internal relationship to concrete events. This means that a criticism of perceptions will be clues to the meaning of experience itself, and not only a projection of one's desires.

Locke reinstated the role of the senses as a stimulus to reflection, and thus, in a way, brought body and mind into a working correlation which required attention to the two sides of life. Experience in its sensory aspects was thus seen to be productive of ideas, though the further process of reflecting upon them was seen to be formative and fulfilling of their implications.[16]

One reason for a critical awareness of perceptions and interests is that this awareness contains clues to the structure of meaning and value. The ideas and feelings that come to consciousness when we attend to experience provide data whereby we can perceive the deeper meanings that are really there.

On the other hand, lived experience does not require any particular interpretation. Lived experience carries multiple meanings. Any response to experience will inevitably be a response to less than the fullness of experience itself. Therefore, every response is a distortion of experience that reveals as much about one's own perspective and interests as it does about the nature of experience itself. The critical nature of practical theology requires that a community become aware, as much as possible, of the relativity of its perspectives and the biases and self-interests that these perspectives protect and enhance.

Habermas and the critical school of Frankfort have been leaders in showing how personal and social interest determines the knowledge that comes from analysis of experience.[17] They suggest that psychoanalysis, with its experience in tranference and counter-transference, is a good model of uncovering personal self-interest. Counter-transference refers to the distortions that a therapist brings to the therapeutic context. These distortions block perception of empirical data and reduce these data to one's own desires and interests. Habermas suggests that we need similar theories of social interest, that is, ways to become aware of the socio-economic interests that are embedded in our perceptions. Given the multiplicity of contexts within which experience is perceived and the relativity of all particular perspectives, practical theology needs a number of critical principles to help us become more aware of the distortions we project. We need ways to critique our intimate relationships, our cultural bias, our gender bias, our bias of privilege, and many others.[18]

In summary, a credible practical theology for the modern world must be a critical theology. In this context, critical means the ability to see one's own perceptions as relative and tentative and the ability to make a radical criticism of one's perspective, in order to use such critique both to enhance perception of reality (lived experience) and to become aware of the self-interests and distortions that are a part of perception itself.

The third step in practical theology is a correlation of perspectives from culture and the Christian tradition.

As soon as one tries to describe some part of lived experience in any self-critical way, one becomes aware of competing systems of interpretation. In local congregations, seminaries, or universities, Christians are faced with structured theories about the important data that one should perceive and the meaning of these data. Perception and interpretation are organized not just by the stories that form the perspectives of persons and communities, but by organized systems of thought and language. Each of these systems, whether religious or secular in content, to the extent that it is represented by a living community of interpretation, represents a claim on the attention of an enlightened group or individual. Every community must have some method for discussing and adjudicating these competing claims to truth and meaning. At this point, we basically accept the method of critical correlation as described by Tracy and Browning. Whether one fits the type of scientific, correlational, or confessional theology, there is a point in the method of each when some correlation between the various Christian and other perspectives is required. The difference between the three types depends on the time and energy spent on this step, rather than its presence or absence. Barth features the importance of confession and tends to place the correlation with other perspectives in the footnotes. Victor Turner features his science and brackets the more theological discussion. But both assume a correlation, and they are aware of choices they are making within that correlation. We believe that the correlational step must be featured in order to deal with the complex issues that are involved here.

Tracy defines theology as "the discipline which articulates mutually critical correlations between the meaning and truth of an interpretation of the Christian fact and the meaning and truth of an interpretation of the contemporary situation."[19] In this definition, Tracy holds up several aspects which are important for this step of practical theology.

First, the community must engage in a hermeneutic of the Christian tradition. There is no single interpretation of the meaning and truth of the story of the Scriptures. Canon theory is showing how the faith communities have systematically preserved a multiplicity of interpretations within the very texts that give us access to our tradition.[20] One task of theology is to articulate a coherent and adequate interpretation of the Christian tradition for the contemporary community. The Christian story is not *an* interpretation of experience. Rather, it is a multiplicity of interpretations with which any particular community must struggle to make its own interpretation in such a way that it can be open to God's surprises in the present and the future. The Christian story in the Bible and the history of the church and its thought is a rich resource of symbols and metaphors for understanding the character of God and God's relationship with particular persons and communities. Continued study of the texts that embody this story is required to keep our own structures alive and vital. Christian life today has continuity with the lives of all those who have tried to be loyal to the Christ. We know who we are by continuing to research and rehearse together these stories within the social and historical contexts in which they have had meaning.

One can see here the potential complexity of the task of practical theology. In order for a community to interpret the meaning of its common experience or correlate its perspectives with others, it must engage in its own hermeneutic of the Christian story to uncover the tradition that shapes its identity. Failure to do this will result in an acculturated community whose identity is only secondarily informed by the Christian tradition.

Fortunately, no particular community is the first to attempt the hermeneutical task, nor is it alone. There is a history of interpretation and there are scholars whose specialization is the exploration of the texts and the contexts of the tradition. However, each community must engage in exploration of the primary data of the tradition and not become overly dependent on secondary sources. Here, we agree with Fowler that the task of practical theology includes more than the use of interpretations from academic theology. It includes interpretation of the texts themselves within the larger theological dialogue.[21]

The second aspect of the correlational step involves a hermeneutic of interpretations from the culture. Examination of "common human experience" in the contemporary culture has resulted in a multiplicity of interpretations. This is one of the meanings of pluralism in the modern world. The variety of interpretations is not chaotic. Rather, the available interpretations are structured into traditions which have their own horizons of normative value. These "horizons of meaning"[22] are not necessarily evident in the claims made by particular interpretations (social or natural sciences). The world view and normative claims of any particular interpretation of common human experience must be uncovered and stated as a part of the process of a correlation of meanings. This means careful study of the assumptions and philosophical context of a science. One could easily spend a lifetime plumbing the depths of modern psychoanalytic theory, for example, without assurance that one had exhausted the possible meanings revealed there, not to mention the task of a correlation. One of the tasks of a community is to engage in such a process of hermeneutics.

The third aspect involves the correlation itself. We accept Tracy's definition of this task as philosophical and metaphysical.[23] In order to correlate two competing perspectives, one must be able to move to a level of abstraction that is similar in both perspectives. For perspectives that are competitive in a fundmental way, this will involve a difference in world view, or in the way that each system makes certain fundamental assumptions about the nature of experience itself. There are simpler and more complex ways to carry on this discussion. A local congregation is engaging in a philosophical discussion whenever it attempts to correlate perspectives that seem mutually contradictory. Nevertheless, some form of abstract, academic philosophy is also appropriate on behalf of the church by persons trained in this science in order to draw out the implications of choices facing Christians in the world today.[24] One must not claim a greater role for this process than is warranted, but there are moments when such a metaphysical correlation is critical to the development of theology and to the future *praxis* of the Christian community.[25]

This is the point at which philosophical theology makes its greatest contribution, and it is important for specialists to be working in this area on behalf of the church. However, all practical theology has a moment which is fundamentally philosophical and which cannot be avoided without being arbitrary. The Christian community is called on to state its perspective as a claim to meaning and to give a reasoned defense of this claim (apologetics). The validity of this process does not depend on its acceptance in the secular world any more than the validity of any other perspective requires popular acceptance. However, the Christian community must be prepared to state its stance and defend it as at least *one* valid perspective on the modern world. While there will be times and places when this defense is ineffective (for example, Germany in 1940), one hopes for some openness in the secular world where such an endeavor makes sense to others. Christians should take advantage of such opportunities with a proper humility about possible success and a willingness to be confessional.

In summary, the correlation step in practical theology has three phases: (1) a hermeneutic of the Christian story, (2) a hermeneutic of interpretations from the culture, and (3) a critical correlation of these interpretations with one another by an analogical method. The result will be systematic theological statements that are informed by cultural perspectives, that arise out of a particular community, and that state its claims in language accessible to the public arena. Thus, the correlation step is philosophical in its method and public in its direction as it attempts to state a Christian perspective on experience in a rational mode.

The fourth step in practical theology is interpretation of meaning and value.

There is a confessional moment in practical theology which cannot be reduced to a science. As valuable as the correlation step is, there is a radical relativity to every perspective which demands rigorous honesty about the confessional component. We take our clue from Daniel Day Williams.

Empiricists have characteristically sought to get beyond the confessional position to explore the realities which are open to human inquiry, and have denied claims to knowledge which have only a private or parochial status. I fully share this concern, but I do not believe in the existence of a purely non-confessional interpretation of human experience and the meaning of God. We live in historical communities of valuation and faith. We see from perspectives informed by primordial and historically embodied value judgments. . . . The fact that we are always within a structure of thought and evaluation does not mean that we are bound to the place from which we start. We are free to criticize and reconsider every claim. It is the empiricists who have insisted on this openness in any confessional position, and I accept it while continuing to hold that every theology is shaped within some community of faith.[26]

Every statement of faith and meaning is relative to a perspective; the potential interpretations of meaning are various. The correlation step points to the need for communities to work together for a public consensus on structures of meaning that provide cohesion for the community and release creativity among its members. But there is a point at which reason fails in its necessity and the community must confess its faith without the assurance of clear logic and total coherence. At this point there is always more research that can be done, more data to be collected, more viewpoints to consider. But the time comes when the community must say, "enough," and courageously make its confession.

A second imperative for the confessional moment is the richness of experience itself. Meland has been most articulate in pointing to the depth of the unconscious experience that cannot be captured by rational thought. One reason is the overwhelming amount of data that is available for thought. Another reason is the limitation of perception itself, which organizes our thinking without full awareness of the context of experience. A third reason is the mystery of God's activity within experience. There is a perverse human tendency to try to domesticate God by our conscious rational constructs. But God's action transcends all our thought about God. Meland suggests that we pay much more attention to the myths of culture and the symbols that disclose transcendent meaning. Human rationality often tends to move toward a clarity that is one-dimensional and out of touch with the ambiguous and unmanageable concrete events in our experience.[27]

There is a moment in all theology when one stands in fear and awe of the depth and mystery of experience. Our rational thought cannot protect us from this moment. It is the existential moment when the community must risk all in order to be faithful to God. It is the moment when we stand before God's direction in our lives. There are greater and lesser degrees of risk, but embedded in every confession is the acknowledgment that one is no longer in control and that one is vulnerable in the presence of an Other that cannot be fully understood. It is at this moment that the community confesses its faith and trusts its life in an elemental way to God.

Ricoeur's distinction of hidden and apparent meaning is helpful here.[28] After rational thought has enlarged perception, there are yet deeper levels of meaning which can only be described by symbol and narrative. Symbolic language is language that discloses the multiple and hidden meanings in experience. Symbols lack precision and clarity, and have deep ambiguity. But they are often the most appropriate language to point to a depth in experience which scientific language cannot touch.

A discussion of the gap between "is" and "ought" also belongs here. While the continuity and discontinuity of descriptive and normative statements is heavily debated,[29] this moment of interpretation emphasizes their discontinuity. Every descriptive statement has a normative horizon, and therefore "is" and "ought" can never be fully separated. Every gesture demands a response, but it can never fully determine which response. There is a freedom of response that can never be eliminated, and it is the response which determines the final meaning of a gesture.[30] Perhaps the gap between "is" and "ought" can never be fully bridged. There is always a confessional element. This means that every normative statement contains the question, Why couldn't it be otherwise? And there are always choices, values, and obligations which have no causal necessity to them. This moment highlights the confessional nature of interpretation and evaluation.

One proponent of interpretation as the critical moment in practical theology is Charles Winquist. He suggests that a major difficulty of much modern human life is a one-dimensional perception that loses touch with the depth of life. The role of religion is to provide the settings and symbols that can lead to conversion, to a new consciousness of the richness of experience. "The need to discover a depth that does not disappoint the new expectations originating in a glimpse of transcendence becomes a central theme of religious life." There is often a basic discontinuity between surface experience as evident in daily life and the transcendent depths of experience. This discontinuity cannot be crossed by logic and coherent rationality. Rather, experience must be broken open by experiences that include "an element of paradox and surprise." Surface experience and one-dimensionality is broken open by symbols which can be fearful and liberating. "The discovery of the symbol is a crack in the surface of experience. This crack is threatening when we are satisfied with the depth that we have achieved in our understanding." But the symbol is also the entry into a deeper consciousness that includes the reality of God as "that than which nothing greater can be conceived" (Anselm), and "the object of our ultimate concern" (Tillich). "The symbol is a coincidence of meanings that generates a gain in consciousness by naturally entertaining contrasts in its simplest expression, . . . The symbol is a bearer of new consciousness and new experience." Part of theology is interpretation. Such interpretation is other than the logical correlation of rational constructs. Interpretation involves disturbing the surface of consciousness through the use of symbols that are multivalent and therefore point beyond present consciousness to a new consciousness. The ministry of interpretation involves three steps, according to Winquist: (1) "ministry accepts the givenness of experience," (2) ministry must "issue an invitation to share in a more satisfying vision of what is real and important in our lives," and (3) ministry "draws from the tradition and history the symbols and mythological ideas that are necessary for the extension of consciousness in the creation of the spirit."[31]

Such a confessional interpretation of human experience highlights certain facets and subordinates others. It gives high value to some features and lesser value to others. It suggests the manner in which God has been present and the direction of God's will. The account offers basic metaphors and analogies within which obligations, intentions, purposes, consequences, causes, and responsibilities are assessed. The analogical and narrative unity between past, present, and future events is suggested. The interrelatedness of cause and purpose moving from past to future through human interaction and commitments becomes visible in the account. Such an evaluative account discloses the faith stance of the one who gives it, but that stance is intimately a part of God's larger purposes in events. Those who hear with any self-investment are similarly challenged as to their relationship to such an evaluative account.[32]

In summary, interpretation and evaluation is the critical step in this model of practical theology. There is much background work that is crucial to the task of interpretation and evaluation, including careful description, rigorous criticism of perceptions, and a correlation of perspectives. But this is preparation for the work of interpretation, which is confession of meaning and testimony to the present activity of God. There is a rational discussion we can have about the forms and styles of interpretation. But a community cannot avoid the personal and communal risk of a confession that has no necessity and is relative to a perspective in a radical way. This is the leap of faith, the willingness to risk oneself for one's beliefs, the courage to be who and where one is before a transcendent God.

The fifth step in practical theology is community critique of interpretation.

Because of the relative and confessional nature of every interpretation, it demands criticism. To go uncriticized would mean to accept one's interpretation as arbitrary and unquestioned. Here, we return to the thought of Habermas that every interpretation contains a personal and social self-interest that must be uncovered. This does not mean that self-interest can be totally exorcised, but interpretations must be as inclusive of lived experience as possible, and criticism of one's interests allows interpretation to be enlarged to include interests besides one's own. Thus, the heart of this step is a critical evaluation of the community interpretation from perspectives other than one's own. What are these other perspectives? The possible particular perspectives are infinite, but we will suggest three types.

91

First, the community must ask if the interpretation is appropriate to persons with various developmental needs and at various levels of maturity. Children need a secure environment in which to develop and test their powers without being traumatized by a malevolent environment. Adolescents need alternative value systems in which they can test their identities. Adults need persons and communities to care for. At all these levels, persons mature through crisis and transition as more and more of their experience becomes available for integration. A community should evaluate its interpretation in terms of some model of maturity and development.

Second, the community must ask if the interpretation is liberating for persons and communities in the world. A narrow, self-serving interpretation will benefit some persons at the expense of others: male over female, white over black, rich over poor. A liberating interpretation will lead to a deeper sense of unity, creativity, and mutuality for all persons and communities. A liberating interpretation will show sensitivity to oppression in its various forms and will seek social change to alleviate this oppression.

Third, the community must ask if the interpretation is sufficiently rich in its symbolism about the depth of life, or whether it narrows perception about life. An interpretation with depth will recognize the ambiguity of concrete experience and will not shrink from the shadow that is always lurking there with its demonic possibilities for novelty or evil. An interpretation with depth will provide powerful cultural symbols which disclose rather than limit the richness of life.

The sixth step in practical theology is the development of guidelines and specific plans for a particular community.

Academic theology has tended to consider its systematic work done at the point of interpretation of the meaning of experience in the modern world.

However, the empirical principle does not allow one to stop reflecting at the most abstract level. A. N. Whitehead says that obtaining knowledge is like a flight of an airplane: One begins on the ground of concrete experience, then one soars into the imagination where coherence and logic are the sole criteria. But one must again land in concrete experience to test the applicability and adequacy of one's speculations.[33] Refusal to return to experience leaves one's ideas floating in thin air where they may have striking coherence and clarity, but they may be irrelevant to real life. Much criticism has come to academic theology from the church because of this problem. But the reason for returning to experience is methodological. By returning to experience, one's ideas can be revised and corrected to reflect the depth of experience. According to the empirical principle, experience is the criterion for knowledge. Abstractions and generalizations are necessary to uncover the structures of meaning within experience. But they must be held in a tentative way and continually checked within experience itself. This means coming down from the thin air of abstraction to the level of concrete thinking. Within practical theology this means the development of guidelines and specific plans for a particular community.

The development of guidelines and plans can move in either a more intuitive or a more pragmatic direction. The intuitive approach attempts to develop guidelines for practice from the evaluative vision of the previous step. Such guidelines then lead to certain procedures. The alternate approach is more pragmatic. In the latter case one formulates the values of the previous step into specific objectives or alternatives. One then selects one alternative, acts upon it, and then examines the results of one's action in terms of the assumed objective and value.

James Gustafson has suggested what he calls a

discernment approach.[34] In Gustafson's view, both the application of principles and the testing of alternative procedures should be considered in terms of the wider context and narrative account of the event. Certain procedures may follow upon the obligations one feels. A group may want to test various alternatives. Such considerations should always be made in view of the evaluative narrative. We believe Gustafson's view is very much in keeping with the movement of practical theology from steps four and five to step six, as we have described them above. Therefore, both inductive and deductive reasoning are appropriate in developing guidelines for practice, but such guidelines should always be considered in view of the wider context of meaning and value.

Browning's approach to the ethics of pastoral care represents a more intuitive approach. Browning is working on method in ethics which moves from the most abstract to the most concrete level. He identifies five levels that must be considered when making this move. The community discussion begins with story and metaphor, the most general and abstract statement about its identity and mission. Then the community discussion moves to the level of obligations, where one identifies the normative principles that have claims on everyone. Next are statements about the needs and values of persons that provide the potentialities and limitations within which the community must work. Then one identifies the contexts within which specific behaviors become important. Finally, there is the level of rules and roles that govern the particular behaviors that are appropriate. Thus, Browning is developing an ethical method that moves from interpretation to specific behaviors in a systematic way that is clear about the various levels of rationality that are involved.[35]

Most planning and administrative theories represent a

more pragmatic approach to practical theology. They usually work from felt needs that arise from experience of the more immediate past. The first step is the celebration of goals which are the most general statement of what a community wants to accomplish. From this, one develops specific objectives which state in more concrete terms the behavioral outcome that is desired. Then one must identify the resources and leadership that are needed to meet these objectives. Finally, one develops a step-by-step strategy that will implement the program and provides for methods of evaluation in order to test the adequacy of one's plans and provide the data for future planning. We have here a method for moving from the abstract level of goals to the concrete behaviors needed to meet these goals. This provides a grounding of goals in concrete experience, and a way of testing the adequacy of one's goals within experience.

The theory-praxis discussion has relevance here. Advocates of a praxis basis for theory demand that all reflection begin and end in praxis. Praxis requires the elaboration of theory, and theory has no purpose except the formation of more praxis. Groome eleborates a method of practical theory based on shared praxis.[36] In that Groome keeps the evaluative context and story constantly in view, his view seems amenable to Gustafson's discernment. However, Groome does not give much guidance as to how such praxis is developed other than to say it is dialectically related to the biblical story and vision.

Recently Rodney Hunter made an important suggestion about what he calls "practical knowledge." He distinguishes practical knowledge from descriptive knowledge that "tells about what is," and normative knowledge that "tells what ought to be." In distinction, practical knowledge "gives information about how to do things." All three kinds of knowledge are reciprocally related to one another, but none is reducible to another. In simpler matters, mere technique is often sufficient. But in complex matters involving the formation of persons and leadership in community, a much more complex kind of practical knowledge is required. "The phrase 'wisdom of experience' instead suggests a form of knowledge that has accrued and matured through a history of practical contingent events."[37] This kind of knowledge cannot be reduced to descriptive or normative forms; rather, it must be learned "by experience."

This fact in turn makes for certain difficulties in acquiring and transmitting it, especially in its more complex forms, because what is learned through experience is to a certain extent, sometimes to a very large extent, specific to particular practitioners or communities of practice. In a certain sense one must be an insider, a practitioner oneself, disciplined by practice, in order to acquire it. Hence, its acquisition and development always involve something like practice, apprenticeship, or discipleship.[38]

This definition of practical knowledge is what theological education has generally meant by "skills" or "arts of ministry." But two things have conspired to make these terms inadequate. One is the sense that they are merely techniques which anyone can learn without significant effort, or arts which cannot be learned at all, but are innate to talented individuals. The second problem is that the skills have been seen as essentially independent of theology itself, either as "means" for the "ends" that theology identifies, or neutral in their theological import. Hunter asserts that there is a form of knowledge called practical knowledge which is not reducible to academic knowledge and which has theological content, since how something is done in the context of personal and community formation is as important as whether it is done. We differ with Hunter at the point of identifying all of practical theology as "practical knowledge."[39] In our view, Hunter's practical knowledge is only one phase of the task of practical theology that begins with description and proceeds through correlation and interpretation in addition to developing the practical knowledge necessary to embody the will of God in concrete situations. However, we believe that Hunter has identified in a fresh way a particular moment in practical theology that certain specialists have stubbornly continued to develop even when its theological content was not clear.

In summary, the last step in practical theory is the development of guidelines and specific plans for a particular community. This means the development of guidelines for practice in view of metaphorical and evaluative descriptions of previous events and of the tradition. The purpose is to find the guidance to return to experience. We have identified three different ways of conceiving of this task: Browning's intuitive method, the pragmatic method of organizational and development theory, and Hunter's practical knowledge. In our judgment, each has a certain legitimacy when carried out with what Gustafson calls discernment. Any and all of them can be carried out within a longer metaphorical and evaluative narrative of the wider context within which the action is being developed. To act in terms of such narrative awareness, which is born of previous experience and of searching one's tradition, is to act in the hope of discerning God's will. The confessional element in the earlier steps is now carried to this step. The creating, forgiving, renewing activity of God becomes the context within which particular guidelines are developed.

Conclusion

We conclude this section on the description of the six steps in practical theology by adding a short note about the content of practical theology within our perspective. The phrase which has captured our imagination is "the formation of persons and communities of faith for the mission of Jesus Christ." The last part points to the importance of understanding our identity in relation to God's action in the life and death of Jesus within the context of the Scriptures and the early church. Even though we are all children of the modern world, with its difficulties and possibilities, our personal and corporate identity is found in the story of Jesus as the Christ to which we continue to try to be loyal.

Within the story of God's action in Jesus, our task is the formation of persons and communities of faith. God's present action is the creation of persons and communities of such quality that the contradictions and evils of this life can be absorbed without the loss of integrity. Peace in the world is a vision, but not a fact. What God wants and works for is a kind of harmony on this globe that can hold and encourage the creativity of all people. Such a vision includes great risk and deep ambiguity, but it is the meaning of God as Jesus proclaimed it.

Our task as leaders in the church and culture is to appropriate the symbols, the ideas, and the skills that may lead to the formation of God's kingdom. This means a kind of personal and communal maturity that can be open to the depths of experience in all its complexity, ambiguity, and threat, and can also act courageously in communion with God's spirit. It requires both passive and active discernment about what God is doing, and an ability to know when to wait on God's initiative and when to act in concert with God's will. It requires an ability to be self-critical in our own perspective, to acknowledge our tendency to distort, and yet the ability to receive forgiveness and courageously confess our belief. It requires the ability to use our rational minds to the limit, and also to stand in awe as a creature before the Creator. It requires an ability to lead the community at appropriate times and to allow others to lead us. It means, while acknowledging ever alienating and destructive possibilities, continuing to believe and to join in the adventure of God's creation and its glorious future.

F O U R

Guidelines for
the Practice of Ministry

In chapter 1 we argued that community is a highly appropriate metaphor for the practice of theology. The church is a living community whose practice is a part of an ongoing and constantly reinterpreted story.

In chapter 2 we distinguished between those practical theologies that are primarily directed to the church and those primarily directed to the wider cultural community. Each of those pairs may in turn be divided into three parts. One pair is guided by some secular discipline of analysis such as psychology, sociology, or anthropology. Another pair is guided primarily by confessional or doctrinal disciplines. A third pair is guided by the dialogue between confessional and secular disciplines. We thereby have distinguished six subtypes of practical theology.

In chapter 3 we suggested a method of doing practical theology. It occurs within the community and begins with describing actual practice. It moves through disciplined analysis of the practice and exegesis of Scripture to a theologically informed vision. It proceeds to a moral evaluation, practice, and re-narration of the ministry process.

This way of describing ministry lifts out community formation as the primary task of ministry. Community formation takes place in the politics of community life as an unfolding story. Community formation in its fullness is marked by the values of creativity, justice, intimacy, and faith. (The characteristic marks of community will be developed further in chapter 5.)

Guidelines for Practice in the Tradition

The medieval church developed the tradition that the bishop is the church and that the sacrament is only properly done through a clergy whose authority is given by the bishop. People were joined to the church through the sacrament and through the moral guidance of the clergy, which guidance was administered primarily through the sacrament of confession. The clergy had authority to require acts of penance, and their moral guidance was decisive. In the medieval church the community was formed primarily through sacrament, administration, and moral guidance. The community was visibly present in the clerical hierarchy and the sacramental presence.

The Reformation began with Luther's attack upon the sacrament of confession. Arguing that only Christ has the power to forgive sins, he called for a new, more immediate relationship of every believer to God's grace in Christ. Preaching and sacrament, as revised, became the source of community.

Pietism, which began in Germany and spread to England, gave rise to small communities of Bible study, spiritual nurture, and evangelism. These communities were understood to be capable of bringing to life a church that had become lost in discussions about theological niceties. From Pietism came the modern mission and education movements as well as modern revivalism. The sources of community come in confession, spiritual nurture, and evangelism.

101

The church in modern America understands all of the following to be related to community formation: sacrament and worship, preaching, care and counseling, mission and evangelism, nurture, education, catechesis, administration, advocacy, liberation, and social action. All of these perspectives on community have important links with the Christian tradition. Each particular denominational tradition evaluates some as more important than others. Part of the contemporary problem is that the multiplicity of possibilities is in itself fragmenting.

The Local Nexus of Practice

We have suggested that practical theology is a search for meaning and value within the interaction and shared loyalties of actual communities. Therefore, practical theology is properly attendant to the actual practice of local congregations. In the decisions of local congregations and their pastors, one glimpses practical theology the way it is actually done. Of course, congregations are linked together in larger ecclesial bodies, but again practical theology is done in reference to and within those larger ecclesial relationships.

In what follows we offer the stories of a number of congregations and their pastors in actual ministry events. Our accounts will suffer from summarization of the rich description that could be given. Nevertheless, they may help to locate the actual setting within which our manifesto for practical theology in the local church takes shape. Each of these stories has been written up in fuller form by a pastor, and they may be obtained by the interested reader. The descriptions themselves have been somewhat fictionalized by changing names, places, and details. However, the narratives describe events that have actually occurred.

Equipping the Saints

The Wheathill congregation[1] is located in a small town in rural Virginia. It is a congregation of some three hundred members, strongly loyal to the denomination and desirous to be faithful Christians. Pastor James Brown is an intense young man whose seminary education and clinical pastoral training has instilled in him a desire to build up the relationships among the people he serves.

Pastor and congregation both felt a need for church renewal. They needed to become more of a ministering congregation by overcoming the gap between clergy and laity. Out of these concerns the people encouraged the pastor to develop a focus upon training for lay pastoral care. The pastor proposed a class of ten two-hour sessions to meet twice a month. "Lay Pastoral Care" proved to be too pretentious, and so Pastor Brown changed the name to "Classes in Lay Ministry," a topic to which more people could relate. Ten persons showed up for the first session, but this dropped off to a regular attendance of nine.

The approach of the class was to carry out ministry under pastoral supervision. Pastor Brown hoped for each person's self-discovery, sense of service, and sense of being related to a ministering community. The focus was not to be on a right or wrong way of doing things.

During each session the group visited a home for the elderly and then returned to reflect on their experiences. They saw themselves directly carrying out the injunction, "I was sick and you visited me" (Matt. 25:36). The pastor understood himself to be equipping "the saints for the work of ministry" (Eph. 4:11-12). During the mutual reflection period after the visits, the group also studied Reuel Howe's *Man's Need and God's Action* (Seabury Press, 1953).

Under the leadership of Pastor Brown, the group interpreted ministry as a mutual activity. Because we are social beings, none of us can completely care for himself/herself entirely alone. The miracle of caring is that in caring for another, one also cares for oneself. The group concluded that to care and to be cared for are not two separate acts. They are both elements of the same process.

Together the lay study group and the pastor developed guidelines for the visitations. The visitors were to focus their attention upon the needs of the other persons. They were to be willing to share their own faith in appropriate ways. They were to be aware of their own feelings about sickness, aging, and death.

The visitors had many kinds of experiences. On one occasion an elderly woman told two visitors, "Get the hell out of my room!" Not knowing how she meant it, they risked staying. As they talked further, they discovered a lonely older person who wanted and needed company, but who protected herself against loneliness by anger and profanity. They had a warm conversation, and she invited the two visitors back again.

As the group evaluated these and other experiences together, they discovered how one of their number tended to dominate others. Someone else tended to be too absorbed in her relationship with others. Still another was grieving over the loss of her grandmother. They not only evaluated the visits with the elderly, they also began to hear and support one another.

Looking back over the experience, some in the study group commented that they had learned to listen more closely than before. Someone discovered that it is better to speak more honestly, not simply to agree to all that is being said. Another felt that he was "finally learning to understand the Bible a little." Someone commented, "My views of life and God have changed." Still another felt that she had become better able to cope with problems of trying to be helpful to someone else.

The pastor and the group concluded the ten weeks' study believing they had touched a central theme in the New Testament, that of equipping the saints for the work of ministry. They saw themselves as "bearers of the light and hope," and "bearers of one another's burdens." Jesus' admonition, "I was sick and you visited me," was embodied for them. To some extent, the laypersons had begun to see themselves as part of the ministry of the church. The pastor's concluding comment was, "The program itself was not without fault, but at least a beginning."[2]

Aiming at Spiritual Growth

Robert Risden is the pastor of First Presbyterian Church in rural Illinois.[3] The congregation is about three hundred in size and Pastor Risden has been there about three years. He and the Session agreed that they needed to take more responsibility for the direction of the church program. During the previous several years, things had moved along informally, and many people were beginning to feel that there should be more focus in the church's program.

Beyond the need for focus, the pastor came to believe that the Session shares responsibility with the pastor for spiritual leadership in the church. In his judgment, program urgencies can too easily overcome the need for spiritual enrichment. His reading of the Reformation ideal was that leadership in the church should embody both spiritual guidance and mutual caring for one another. John Wesley developed "bands," classes and societies for mutual edification, and fraternal correction of one another.

When the pastor's concern was discussed by the

Session, they agreed that the Session should be more intentional about encouraging the vitality of the faith of church members. Furthermore, the spirituality of the congregation tends to reflect that of church leaders, so Session members should give attention to growing together in faith. The Session decided to become more aware of one another's faith and to study together the meaning and purpose of the church. Out of their faith sharing and study, they hoped to set goals and establish priorities for the future direction of the congregation.

The Session then began a course of study using the book *Living the Adventure* (Word Books, 1975) by Bruce Larson and Keith Miller, a course that met weekly for three months. Each of the members took turns leading the group for one evening. Furthermore, they held extended retreats before and after the three-month course of study. During the three months, Pastor Risden had at least one conversation with each Session member regarding that person's faith.

At the conclusion of the course of study, Session members were enthusiastic about how much closer they felt to one another. They agreed that they felt a much greater sense of community as a result of the study and discussion. They also felt that they had developed better patterns of working together. They felt more free to express faith and personal concerns in the group than they had before.

However, when asked about the quality of their faith, most responded that they saw little change. The pastor's interpretation of the surprising response was that as one becomes more reflective about faith, one may become more self-critical about one's own faith. The group's answer to this question seemed to belie the pastor's perception that there was actual growth in faith among participants. Perhaps growth in faith is not a reasonable expectation for such a program. Perhaps the freedom to express one's faith is far easier to achieve during such a course of study.

After the study experience, one person commented, "This has been a tremendous growing year for the Session." In a more reserved style, another person wrote, "I feel our Session has grown spiritually this past six months." Someone else commented about being able "to take a close look at our own faith as well as gain some understanding of the faith of others." Even the most skeptical member of the group, who insisted that he still is not willing to enter into this kind of open group process, nevertheless wrote, "I cannot help but be impressed by the profound effect this experience has had on those in the group who did subscribe fully."

The final retreat saw a number of actions taken by the Session. They decided to restructure Session meetings to include study and personal sharing as well as committee reports and business items. They also decided to continue their study of the marks of the church so they would have more adequate criteria by which to judge their own work together. Interestingly, they decided to redistribute committee appointments so that more persons beyond the Session could be included. The redistribution of committee assignments was also intended to yield the additional time necessary for study and sharing of faith. Finally, the group agreed to establish an annual retreat for planning and goal setting.

The pastor later commented that neither he nor the Session members could have predicted such positive results from the "hesitant and tentative" beginning of the program.[4] He began to see changes in other areas of the church program. Spirituality was becoming much more central to church programming. The nominating committee began to consider spiritual sensitivity in presenting a slate of officers. The pastor felt confirmed in his original idea that a change in the faith experience of those responsible for the mission of the church can have dramatic effects for the whole congregation. He and the Session both came to a strong conviction that business decisions and spiritual awareness belong to one another in the life of the church, and especially with those who are charged with leadership.

Evangelism as Hospitality

Andrew Fredrick knew that the Terrytown congregation should be more evangelistic.[5] It was often mentioned in business sessions and private conversations. Terrytown was a congregation of about two hundred fifty members, located in a small town in rural western Ohio. For the past several years they had held evangelistic services coupled with a neighborhood canvass. However, very few members of the church took part in the effort, and even fewer outsiders became interested in the church as a result of the half-hearted efforts. No one was surprised. They did not really see themselves as an evangelistic church. They knew that evangelism belongs to the gospel, but that was not enough genuinely to motivate people.

Noticing an article on the subject of hospitality evangelism in the denominational journal, Pastor Andrew Fredrick passed it on to leaders in the church. The gist of the article was that when a congregation becomes a genuinely hospitable people, those outside the fold are attracted. Hospitality is a central mark of the people of God, and hospitality is enjoined as a virtue throughout the Old and New Testaments. Hospitality can be expressed in a thousand ways, but it features helping people feel "at home" in the congregation.

Under the pastor's direction, a questionnaire was circulated to the congregation to discover what had led them to join the Terrytown congregation. The answers surprised the committee. The respondents mentioned the friendly atmosphere, caring attitudes of members, personal invitations, and being "adopted" by the church family. What did they find most impressive about the Terrytown congregation? The answers: willingness to help those in need, working together, closeness within diversity, freedom to be oneself, and family atmosphere.

They quickly noted that personal invitations were quite different from stereotypic evangelistic campaigns, and that invitations were usually to someone well known to the inviter. The sense of being genuinely invited, genuinely welcomed, and made to feel at home was basic. In a word, the respondents to the questionnaires mentioned attitudes and activities that easily fall under the biblical concept of hospitality.

The newly formed hospitality committee began to dream about what would happen if the church began to practice hospitality on a more intentional basis. The pastor initiated and taught a class on aspects of hospitality within the Gospel of Matthew. From that class came two suggestions. One suggestion was that the pastor lead a Sunday school class of young adults in a study of hospitality in the Scriptures. A second suggestion was that the deacons begin to develop a program of hospitality for the church.

Scriptural study uncovered the Hebrew practice of washing feet, bowing, and preparing a meal as signs of hospitality to visitors. The washing of feet and the meal were a part of Jesus' last supper with the disciples. Historically, both Benedictines and Anabaptists considered hospitality to strangers to be integral to their faith. The stranger was interpreted as a presence of Christ or as the person in need to be served out of obedience to Christ. Both groups struggled with the question of

109

whether preferential treatment was to be given to those within the community or to the stranger (Gal. 6:10).

The young adults began to invite other persons to dinner or to social events such as tennis, racquetball, theater, swimming, picnics—some sponsored by the church and some not. They also began to invite outsiders to worship, and they took the initiative to contact potential members. The deacons began to invite various families for lunch. They developed a program to greet visitors at worship, and they created a listening center where persons with any kind of concern could find someone to talk to.

In a three-month period, the Sunday school attendance increased by 36 percent in comparison to the previous year. Worship attendance was up 19 percent. The pastor became convinced that the practice of hospitality was strengthening the church in its understanding of its calling. The congregation became more open within itself and more able to reach out. Church members commented about the new attitude they found in the church. The congregation began to feel that they were practicing evangelism in a way that fitted their understanding of the gospel.

In reflecting upon their experience in hospitality evangelism, Pastor Fredrick believes that a congregation can intentionally model itself after the biblical practice of hospitality. Bible study and discussion are basic. The actual expressions of hospitality are manifold, easily identified, and require little training. It is a matter of having the courage to risk trusting one another, both within and beyond the church. Since the heart of hospitality is the welcoming of the stranger, it is not limited to "homegeneous grouping" of the same kind of people. Hospitality is rooted deep in Christian tradition and is open to a wide variety of expressions.

Sermons for City Settings

The Withering Spires congregation in a large urban area of Indiana sensed that it was on the decline.[6] When they employed a young woman, Mary Archer, recently graduated from seminary and recently ordained, they hardly dared hope that the decline would cease. However, attendance and other signs of vitality immediately began to increase. Pastor Archer decided that her preaching must be more relevant to the urban context of the congregation. She therefore asked the congregation to assist her in enriching and evaluating the urban relevance of her preaching. Each of the persons she approached quickly agreed to help.

The pastor began by diagnosing her preaching to be too theologically and biblically abstract. She wanted to direct her preaching in a more astute manner to characteristics of the urban setting that were experienced as alienating or stressful. To this end, she asked two groups of people to assist her. The first group, calling themselves "the brainstorming group," met on three different occasions to discuss how the urban setting affected the congregation as a whole as well as each individual. They suggested that the urban realities to be addressed were anonymity, depersonalization, absence of extended families, moving, changing employment, job pressure and stress, and transiency. These urban realities became the focal points for a series of sermons. Her sermon series featured insecurity, stress, community life, mission, and the meaning and purpose of life.

Pastor Archer asked a second group of persons to serve as an evaluation group. These persons were chosen because they were insightful and free to express their criticism. They agreed to fill out questionnaires following each sermon, although they did not meet as a

111

group. They responded to such questions as these: Was the central idea of the sermon identifiable? Was the outline clearly apparent? Was the biblical message clear or obscure? Did the message facilitate spiritual growth? Was the language understandable? Did voice volume and inflection help engage attention? Were there sufficient gestures and eye contact? Was the sermon relevant to this urban setting? In developing these questions, Pastor Archer consulted with other pastors and with persons skilled in questionnaire development.

The evaluation group indicated through the questionnaires that the pastor's sermon series did, indeed, speak to features of the urban situation and to the needs of individuals in the congregation. Comments about the sermon delivery were positive. A number of respondents called for greater clarity in the sermon outline.

Pastor Archer spent much time with a group of other pastors and professional persons evaluating her sermons. In addition to exegetical studies for the sermons, she also studied literature about preaching and about the urban situation. Her study and discussion led her to change her mind radically regarding preaching to human need. She had begun by assuming that her preaching needed greater attention to analyzing the needs of persons within the urban setting. Her study, discussion, and reflection convinced her that sermons must be theologically and biblically profound if they are to touch human need. Harry Emerson Fosdick's model of preaching to human need brought much shallow, trivial preaching in its wake, even though Fosdick himself was able to embody great biblical themes in his preaching. This led Pastor Archer to the conclusion that in every sermon the Scripture must address the congregation.

She developed a greater sense of the sermon as the Word of the Lord. She discovered that her sermons had been primarily didactic and moralistic rather than

112

simply abstract, as she had earlier thought. She decided to make her sermons more kerygmatic. God is in the world, in this urban area, reconciling the world to himself through Jesus Christ.

Within biblical and kerygmatic preaching one can incorporate the needs and concerns of the congregation. From her study she became sensitive to the ways urban Americans are captive to materialism, corporate images of career success, and narcissism. Biblical and kerygmatic preaching does not exclude urban analysis.

She was surprised to discover the positive feelings of many in the congregation toward the urban setting. Urban existence provides a rich diversity of choices and experiences that many found to be liberating. Urban reality provides for a multi-racial and multi-cultural environment that points to the glorious creativity and possibility of God's kingdom. The positive biblical images of the city in Hebrews 11:16 and Revelation 21:2 must not be lost in the more negative images. God's invitation is to accept the inherent joys and pressures of urban living, to see them as the occasion of God's creative, reconciling, and redeeming love.

By engaging the congregation in planning and evaluating sermons, Pastor Archer discovered how helpful it is to become more intentional about including the congregation in the sermon process. The "brainstorming group" was very positive about its contribution to the preaching. The congregation now plans to incorporate talk-back sessions into their worship. Pastor Archer also discovered her own ambivalence about preaching. She had originally been sensitive to the congregation's ambivalence about a woman preacher, but she discovered her own ambivalence. She hopes that this discovery will also help her in preaching the Word of God.

A Revitalized Diaconate

The Trinity Lutheran Church, Missouri Synod, is located in a large urban center in the Midwest.[7] The young pastor's name is Alfred Linter. The congregation is not large, the membership numbering perhaps two hundred fifty. Mr. Linter had been appointed to Trinity several years earlier, and he felt the need to develop a new intensity of ministry in the congregation.

Pastor Linter had believed for some time that the diaconate did not hold a proper place in many Lutheran parishes. His reading of early church history was that deacons were appointed to share both the liturgical and service dimensions of ministry. The lists of duties in I Timothy 3 and II Timothy 2 include service, liturgy, preaching, and administration. During the second century A.D., deacons participated in the celebration of the Eucharist, preaching, distribution of money and food to the needy. By the third century the diaconate was becoming more involved in the liturgical ministry of the church. Duties of church administration ranked second, and a small amount of time was given to service and care of the needy.[8] By the end of the sixth century, the diaconate had become a stepping-stone on the way to the priesthood.

In Pastor Linter's view, the diaconate became of less importance in the medieval period. Its duties became entirely liturgical and the service ministries were taken over by the religious orders. Only among occasional groups like the Bohemians and Waldensians did deacons continue a ministry of service.

With the coming of the Reformation, Luther's emphasis on the priesthood of all believers and faith active in love implied a redress of the balance between liturgy and service in the role of the deacon. However, political and social turmoil during the course of the

Reformation did not support such a change. The development of Lutheran orthodoxy excluded the diaconate, while the development of Pietism tended to give pastoral ministry over to the control of the laity.

Pastor Linter saw the need for the diaconate to share in the ministerial office of both liturgy and service. He found a historical basis for his view in the practice of the early church. He found further substantiation in fundamental doctrines and intentions of Martin Luther, the implications of which have not been carried out. Furthermore, he saw the need for a wider participation of the laity in the office of ministry.

On the basis of his historical and biblical study, and with official approval, he recruited a number of laypeople who were willing to be trained and appointed as deacons. The training consisted of a course of seven sessions. In the first session the pastor summarized the history of the diaconate and introduced the work of being an usher. The second session featured instruction about the diaconal role in baptism and Holy Communion. Next came instruction on public reading of Scripture.

The fourth session was turned to the ministry of service. Behavior during hospital visitation was studied and hospital visits were made. Similar visits to new members and parents of newly baptized persons were studied and carried out. Then came visits to shut-ins and the elderly. The final session dealt with church discipline, the visitation of those who had ceased attending or who had otherwise strained their relationship with the church.

Pastor Linter then taught a series of Bible studies in the Sunday school on the topic of diaconal ministry. He also preached a series of sermons about the relationship of laity to ministry. In bulletins, newsletters, and special announcements, the congregation was kept aware of the newly activated diaconate.

Following the training sessions, the pastor continued to meet monthly with the newly appointed deacons. In these meetings they planned for upcoming worship services, visits to the sick and shut-ins, and discussed what had happened during the deacons' ministry of the previous month.

The focus on the diaconate was well received at Trinity Lutheran. They saw themselves in continuity with the millennia-long practices of the church, and especially the church of their own heritage. They also felt that the ministry was strengthened and deepened in their own congregation.

Meeting Racial Change

Prince of Peace was an old established, white, middle-class congregation in a large urban area on the eastern seaboard.[9] In the late fifties rapid urban change brought an influx of black population. The denomination's annual conference had called upon congregations to declare their intention to minister to all races, so Prince of Peace made such a declaration. Pulpit exchanges with neighboring black churches were initiated and committees were formed to study the situation.

By the early seventies the congregation was searching for a decision. Prince of Peace jointly sponsored a vacation Bible school with a neighboring black congregation. After a race-relationship workshop, the congregation attempted, unsuccessfully, to employ a black staff member. A Seventh-day Adventist group was given permission to use the sanctuary for a year. By the middle seventies there was a sharp decline in membership. A white pastor who had spent several years in a black community development program in rural Mississippi was employed.

116

The congregation turned to James Witter, a denominational consultant who was black. Witter outlined a three-phase program: (1) to develop greater understanding of the situation on the part of the leaders in the congregation, (2) to establish realistic goals for the congregation, and (3) to encourage members and friends of Prince of Peace to commit themselves to the newly formulated goals.

For seven weeks a group of congregational leaders collected and discussed data about the congregation and its community. They resolved to meet more directly the material and spiritual needs of the people by revitalizing worship, making the church school an instrument of evangelistic outreach, developing a number of new choirs, and employing a staff member for community outreach. The church leaders pledged themselves to publicize the new goals and to develop an enlistment and commitment program that would reach all persons related to Prince of Peace. They also decided to ask for district and denominational help to carry out their plan.

The young white pastor volunteered to become the new appointee for community outreach so that a black pastor could be employed. A new black pastor was found, a person who had extensive experience in urban ministry. Very soon a new choir director was appointed and children's, youth, and adult choirs were begun. There followed a tutoring program for elementary school children. A day-care center was also set up. People responded to the enlistment for commitment, and new members began to join the church.

In reflecting on the process, Witter puzzles about how a defeated spirit in a congregation can become vital and hopeful. He sees a congregation that understood itself, however vaguely, to be the household of God, the welcomer of strangers in the name of Christ. They were

117

able to reach out for help, become realistic about their situation, give up the traditions that stood in their way, and to plan in a manner that was insightful and increasingly hopeful. Throughout the process they kept their vision of being faithful to Christ, being a servant to the new creation of God's community, trying new possibilities. Witter saw himself as one who encouraged them to be true to their faith in the face of threatening racial change.

Guidelines for Practice

The brief stories of ministerial practice we have recounted above are actual instances of ministry. They are overly abbreviated and therefore they may glide over crucial events or conjunctions of events that were decisive in the turn of the story. The curious reader can pursue these stories further by consulting the library at Bethany Theological Seminary.

The stories are chosen to illustrate a variety of kinds of ministry in a variety of situations and from various traditions. They describe pastoral care, preaching, administration, evangelism, advocacy, and diaconal ministry. The settings are rural, small town, suburban, and urban. The traditions are Presbyterian, Missouri Synod Lutheran, and Church of the Brethren. The ministry of a woman as well as men is illustrated.

The situations and problems are radically different, but in each case the pastor understands ministry to be a matter of community formation. Pastoral care occurs as people begin to care for one another and gain the courage to reach out in their care for others. Evangelism occurs as people who are strangers within the church become more hospitable to one another and begin to reach out to include those who are outside the fold. Administration occurs within the context of a governing body that discovers how to share their faith with one another. Preaching is more than throwing the Lord's Word to the listener and more than perceiving the listener's need. Preaching includes enabling a community to become aware of their own needs and joys. Preaching attends to God addressing the community through the community's understanding of itself. The diaconate is a traditional way of allowing ministry to be extended from one person to many in the congregation. Social and racial change become a part of ministry as people catch a glimpse of the new possibilities for community formation.

The formation of community was seen in various dimensions of these stories. Ministry began with a consensus and a covenant. In many cases the pastor may have initiated an idea. However, the pastor's view had power to the extent that it was disciplined by his or her carefully listening to the congregation. The ministry proceeded with the development of a consensus. Perhaps not everyone was initially aware that a "brainstorming group" was helping plan the sermons, yet nearly everyone agreed to and supported the process. Establishing the covenant often began with the whole congregation's initial approval, proceeded through disciplined small groups, and then moved out again to the congregation at large. Had strong disagreements arisen, as could have easily happened at the Prince of Peace Church, then the ministerial effort would have moved back again to the process of establishing the covenant.

Covenants may be informal or formal. A congregation may carry out ministry within an informal and assumed agreement about what is worth doing. In each of the stories we have examined, the covenant was formal and expressed. The Wheathill congregation agreed that the pastor should develop a group for lay

119

training. The Withering Spires congregation approved a focus upon congregational involvement in preaching. The Prince of Peace congregation moved along on an assumed agreement to minister to all races, but their decision took on more power when they agreed to seek a consultant and to support the consultant's recommendations. The formal covenant leads to intentional ministry.

Whereas a covenant represents some consensus and commitment within a congregation about the direction of ministry, that covenant cannot take shape until groups and persons accept the continuing embodiment of that covenant. In each of our stories of ministry there were at least three different groups involved. One group represented the continuing concern of the congregation for covenant. In some cases this group was the church board, but not in all cases. A second group was made up of those who carried out the ministry project. For Mary Archer, the "brainstorming group" represented the congregation in helping plan the sermons. For Andrew Fredrick, the young adults' class and deacons sought ways to embody hospitality in the congregation. In Robert Risden's church, the Session fulfilled both the consensus function and the ministry function.

A third set of groups were those with whom the pastor consulted. In each of the stories given, the pastor was related to a group of pastors who could give some alternative perspectives on what he or she was doing. These pastors also sought out supervisors, seminary specialists, denominational consultants, and district pastors to give them help and counsel. In doing so, they drew upon the resources of the larger community within which every local community has its place.

We have been considering the development of a covenant as a precondition and direction for ministry. A second characteristic of all these stories is that the congregation and the pastor sought to become self-critically aware of their situation. In some cases they brought a special secular discipline to bear upon the analysis. Such self-criticism varied from church to church and depended a great deal on the resources available, but such self-critical analysis seems to be decisive.

The Wheathill congregation saw a need to incorporate more laypeople in a ministry of visitation. This assessment was complemented by Pastor Brown's special clinical pastoral education skills that made him especially adept at training his people to be genuinely caring and responsive. The First Presbyterian Church was convinced that the Session needed to do better planning. Pastor Risden's special training and competence in group dynamics helped him to suggest a procedure. The Terrytown congregation was keenly aware of its needs for evangelism. Pastor Fredrick's experience of having wayfarers accepted into his parents' home during the thirties helped him assess what might be done. Mary Archer began with a conviction that she must become more adept at the analysis of human need in the urban situation for her preaching to improve. The Withering Spires congregation saw her effort as hopeful, and they wanted to encourage her in every way possible. Pastor Linter assessed his congregation as needing more ministerial help than he alone could provide. His historical skills allowed him to make a more critical analysis. James Witter proposed to the Prince of Peace congregation that they begin with a seven-week assessment of needs and resources both within the congregation and within the larger community. Witter brought special skills of institutional analysis. In every case, we find a narrative evaluation and assessment of the congregation's situation, often coupled with a disciplined special analysis from the point of view of a secular discipline.

Critical awareness of the situation goes hand in hand with critical awareness of the tradition. In all of our stories of ministry both the congregation and the pastor understood the congregation's story to be within the larger Christian story. The conversation between the congregation's story and the larger Christian story was, in every case, the dynamic from which the vision of ministry took place. There was, if you like, a dialectical hermeneutic between the contemporary story and the Christian story.

Pastor Brown's biblical and theological analysis of the meaning of ministry guided him in setting up a class to train for lay ministry. They saw themselves as extending the story of Jesus and the New Testament community by visiting the sick and helping those in need.

Pastor Risden's reading of Scripture and Christian history was that practical decisions are appropriately made within the context of faith sharing and a spiritual search. The Session then became engaged in a study of the nature of the church, and they decided that they must continue that study to be true to their responsibilities within the Session. Pastor Fredrick and the Terrytown congregation developed their hospitality ministry on the basis of careful Bible study of hospitality as a virtue. Pastor Archer's study of the theology of preaching altered her vision of the meaning of preaching. Alfred Linter's proposal for the diaconate came out of a careful and extended Bible study. At every point in the story, James Witter and the Prince of Peace Church understood themselves to be working within a vision of the kingdom of God. The dialectical hermeneutic between the Chrisian story and the congregation's story is so basic and essential that the stories are inconceivable without it. In nearly every case, there was an ongoing Bible study in which a group was discussing how to address a present existential situation.

In each of our stories of ministry, critical awareness of the situation and the tradition led to focused community planning and expression. There was a moral assessment of the situation, a limited plan of action, a disciplined engagement of the community, an aesthetic expression. Otherwise stated, there was an interplay of the narrative assessment, limited goals and objectives, and functioning groups, and a particular style. The ability to find limited and focused expressions of ministry within a community's unique style is essential to continuing the community's story. Some of the groups were more precise in their objectives and purposes than others, but in each case there were disciplined and uniquely imaginative efforts to give limited scope and focus to the ongoing congregational story of ministry.

James Witter's approach with the Prince of Peace Church was to help the congregation find specific objectives that fit the church's situation and then to marshal the resources to carry out those objectives. From his reading of the need for a service and liturgically oriented diaconate, Pastor Linter set out to recruit a certain number of persons who would be willing to be trained in a program of seven sessions that were carefully designed. Mary Archer proposed a series of five sermons on the urban setting, group discussions, and study. In the process, she completely changed her mind about the place of the analysis of human need in preaching. She found her direction shifting, but within the larger narrative of ministry. Pastor Fredrick worked with two different groups over a period of weeks to help them give their own creative expression to hospitality. Pastor Risden and the First Presbyterian Church engaged in a weekly course of study of a particular book which led them to a particular and unique proposal about how planning should be done in the church. Pastor Brown trained a small group of persons to be

123

good listeners by study and by visiting the elderly over a limited number of weeks. There are many creative ways to give focus to a community's expression of ministry, but without such creative unity of discipline and style the story does not become embodied with power.

In each of our stories of ministry there was a reinterpretation of the community's story and the tradition upon the basis of what occurred. Such a reinterpretation is more than an assessment in view of the initial objectives and more than an indication of whether the process was efficient or effective. Such reinterpretations take account of the creative plans, the disciplined efforts, the unique conjunction of occurrences, the degree to which initial anticipations are met, the changes that occur within persons and groups, the larger meaning of these events, the longer direction of the congregational story, and the continuing interplay with the longer Christian story.

Pastor Fredrick and the Terrytown congregation became convinced that hospitality is a biblically faithful and viable expression of evangelism that fits their own deepest loyalties and customs. Pastor Archer discovered a new meaning of preaching for herself, and the congregation discovered a new way to be engaged in preaching. Pastor Risden and the Session became increasingly convinced that the spiritual search is an integral part of business responsibilities in the church. James Witter and the Prince of Peace congregation together saw that they were able to give up past customs and perceptions to develop a faithful and adventurous program in the face of radical social change. Pastor Brown and the group of lay visitors saw their visits as deeply interrelated to Jesus' instructions to visit the sick and to the admonition in Ephesians "to equip the saints for the work of ministry." Pastor Brown did not know how this story would be continued, but he felt that the efforts were fitting and appropriate in the congregation's ongoing story. Pastor Linter reviewed the establishment of a diaconate by seeing it as a significant and historically faithful model for other congregations. Reinterpretation of the community's story in dialectical interrelationship with the biblical story is the continuing setting within which ministry occurs.

The pastor's role in our stories of ministry has certain features that reach beyond the traditional differences in the office of pastor. Each of the pastors took considerable initiative, but the initiative was responsive to and within the parameters of the community process. The pastors each had their own critical awareness of situation and tradition, their own express plan and style of ministry, their own interpretation of what had taken place. However, their own awareness and expression were always in response to and anticipation of the larger community awareness and expression. They saw ministry as community formation in that they worked to develop and live within ongoing covenants. They led and encouraged the congregation to greater awareness of the situation and the tradition. They helped develop a congregational discipline of interrelating the situation and biblical interpretation in the process of ministry. They encouraged the congregation's own unique expression and style just as they found their own ministry an ongoing adventure and discovery. They also encouraged the congregation in the ongoing reinterpretation of what had occurred in light of a similar reinterpretation of the Scripture's meaning. In a word, they saw themselves a part of ministry as a community process. They were able to take initiative within the interactive process according to their own insight, abilities, and style, but always toward community formation and transformation.

F I V E

Community Formation
as the Task of Ministry

We have developed the theme that "living community" is central to much current conversation among theologians (chapter 2). We have suggested a method whereby a living Christian community can move from described experience, through critical reflection, to interpretations that lead to guidelines for practical life (chapter 3). Then we illustrated our method by referring to ministries in various types of local congregations (chapter 4). In this chapter, we turn to the metaphor of community in order to explore its rich meanings and its implications for a vision of ministry.

Our thesis is that community can be an adequate metaphor for ministry if it is understood with enough complexity and depth, and if it is rooted in the Christian story of God and God's people. We hope to describe community so it can empower the church in its mission in the world.

"Community" has many different meanings, from the intimacy of family and close friends, to the vision of a global community of interdependence.[1] "Community" is a word that often has deep meaning for people, yet its referent is ambiguous. Community refers to the communion that people desire with one another, the deep sense of belonging to one another.[2] Because a

126

sense of belonging is one of the deepest needs of persons, community, as a symbol of that belonging, is an ambiguous symbol. On the one hand, it points to our hopes and dreams for a place in the world that is nurturing and satisfying. As such, it puts us in touch with the mystery of life and our hopes for shared life of meaning and fulfillment. On the other hand, community often represents our dashed hopes and unfulfilled expectations. Where is the community in which we are fully accepted and nurtured and challenged? Our experiences with persons and groups are deeply ambiguous. Our relationships are too often character-ized by betrayal and pain. Consider the impact of divorce on extended families, of dashed expectations between pastor and congregation, of broken treaties and exploitation between nations. Because community is an ambiguous symbol of human dreams and despair, it is not an easy metaphor for ministry.[3]

In the previous chapter, various descriptions of congregational life were given. In each case, someone became concerned about some aspect of the shared life of the people: the spiritual life of its leaders, its relationships to the immediate community, its outreach and evangelism to others. Through discussion with others, this concern came to be shared as an issue for the whole community and a process of study and reflection was begun. Out of the study came an interpretation of the situation and a plan of action designed to engage persons in new shared behaviors.

The result was some change in the shared under-standings and shared patterns of community life. We are suggesting in this chapter that "community" is one of the most helpful metaphors to frame what happened in these stories and it can help us understand more fully ministry in the local congregation and in other levels of community as well. We will use the congregation as one of our major illustrations. However, we believe that the metaphor of community can be extended to include units as small as the individual person and as large as the universe as God experiences it.

One of the primary tensions in the biblical witness to God's life is between the drive toward adventure and the yearning for communion.[4] God's creation of the world and God's continuous interaction with it is an open-ended adventure. God created the heavens and the earth and saw that "it was good" (Gen. 1:10). Like Abraham, God set out on an adventure, the end of which is not totally determined. The direction of this adventure is toward beauty and richness, but its form is yet to be worked out in interaction with his creatures. Yet, there is a deep yearning for harmony and right relationship in this adventure. God has instilled into the creation a deep sense of belonging. "So shall you be my people, and I will be your God" (Jer. 11:4). "I am the vine, you are the branches" (John 15:5).

God's life is a tension between communion and adventure. The drive toward communion pulls all things toward unity and peace. The drive toward adventure risks chaos and disruption for the sake of richness and complexity. Human life is similar. We yearn to belong deeply, but we fear being smothered and constrained by the cost of unity. We press on to use our gifts to the maximum, but fear the isolation and loneliness of individual achievement. Communion and adventure are polarities within community which seem to be at odds, but which call out for one another in our concrete life together. We belong to one another, not as an end in itself, but toward the goal of beauty. We are called to join God's adventure of creation, not alone, but in communion with others. This tension between the sense of belonging and the sense of being separate and unique will underlie much of our discussion.

The Nature of Community

In this section, we will try to define "community" so that it has enough complexity and depth as a symbol to account for the variety and ambiguity of human experience. An assumption of our work is that all human experience is corporate, that it consists of communal events. It is not our intent to give a full definition of the requirements of community itself; that task remains for another time. Rather, we will focus on the question of value within community. How can we recognize community that is becoming more loving according to the biblical vision? How can we tell when certain aspects of community life are problematic and need transformation? How can we interpret community life within the congregation so that God's love can become more manifest and human suffering can be transformed into the energy of faithfulness? In order to respond to these questions, we will suggest a definition of loving community, and then describe and illustrate the various parts of the definition.

Loving community is a process of interaction that moves toward creativity, justice, intimacy, and faith.

Community is a process of interaction within an historical and socio-political context. Interaction is a term for a process view of reality. According to this view, the core of reality, including human experience, is a dynamic process of occasions. "To be concrete, real, effective existence is to be involved in a process of becoming in relation to other entities which also become."[5] The word "interaction" is designed to characterize human experience in dynamic, processive terms. Experience is a process of response to relationships in which one's being is internally constituted by interaction with others.[6]

Communities are not static; they are series of experiences. Individual moments of experience come into being and then pass their lives on to the next moments. What we understand as communities are really many moments of experience which have enduring characteristics. A congregational community is a dynamic organism. Persons exchange gestures with one another in an ongoing sequence that is sometimes predictable, and sometimes unusual. Whenever the people gather, they are in the middle of a flow of experience that extends far into the past and has implications for the future. Every action is a response to what has gone before and an anticipation of a potential future. What we think of as continuity and stability are patterns that are repeated with dependability and, therefore, come to have meaning for all.

Community describes our experience of being involved in a process of interaction with many actors, with continuity to the past, and with a possibility of novelty in the future. When Pastor Risden became concerned about the spiritual growth of his Session, it was in response to a routinization of the business meetings, and in hopes of different behavior and communication in the future. His interpretation was a response to past interaction, and an anticipation of future interaction. It was a moment in the process of interaction we know as community life.

All community interaction occurs within an historical and socio-political context. Each moment of community life has a history, a story. Much has been said in recent literature about the narrative character of human experience.[7] At a basic level, this merely means that experience is cumulative.[8] Each moment in the past has its causal effect on the present and helps determine its possibilities and constraints.[9] Every decision we make attempts to continue some of the trends from the past

130

and redirect others. But the literature on narrative is describing something more. Not only is the past in general important in establishing the context for life, but the particular story which has continuity over time and is remembered and rehearsed in ritual form by its members is a major source of community identity.[10] A nation celebrates its day of independence and its inauguration of leaders in order to sustain its identity as a nation. A congregation studies the Scriptures, worships together, and tells the stories of its denominational and local beginnings in order to remember who it is. In order to understand a particular community, one must know something about the stories it tells and the images of identity that have power for it.

The Levels of Communities

One way to conceptualize the historical and socio-political context of community is in terms of levels. Every community which we can name is already a complex society of societies, that is, it is made up of subgroups with complex interrelationships within a unique history. Likewise, every community is a society within larger societies. Delineating the typical levels of communities in our present world will remind us of the complex interdependence of all things and will help us take care that we identify the level of community on which we are trying to focus. While any list of such communities is arbitrary, the act of making such a list will remind us of complex historical and socio-political context of all community life.

(1) *The Person*

Every individual is a complex system with his or her own unique story, the accumulation of interaction with others and a physiological organism of many sub-societies that is more or less coordinated to deal with the environment; furthermore every person's meaning and integrity is shaped and challenged by interaction with many other communities. The individual is already such a complex society that it merits the study and attention of many kinds of researchers. When we begin to think of the person without clear and distinct boundaries, but as a society made up of many communities and a part of many communities, then human life takes on a much deeper corporate nature than many theories allow. Some parts of human experience are made up of fairly predictable patterns of behavior and can be studied universally, for example, the digestive system in the way it usually handles food and disease.

But other aspects of human experience are unique to the particular story and the particular social location of the person. Meaning and action in this case cannot be understood without careful regard for the context of the person's life. For example, the meaning of a ritual like marriage can only be understood when one explores the historical and socio-political context of that event for particular persons and groups. It will depend on one's unique story, age, stage of development, culture, language. We are learning much about the predictable and repeatable patterns of behavior for individuals. Our thinking about the unique and particular experiences of persons is less developed.

(2) *Systems of Primary Relationships*

Every person is a member of systems of relatives and friends who provide opportunities for face-to-face interaction on a regular basis. Researchers are discovering the impact that these systems have on the experiences and behaviors of individuals. As persons interact with one another over time to accomplish the basic tasks of providing for physical and emotional needs, they develop habitual patterns of interaction. As Mead says, interaction becomes significant as the persons in a social act develop common symbols and meanings and develop similar attitudes. Many of these significant symbols are received from the culture in terms of language and other forms of communication. But many symbols are idiosyncratic to a particular system.

Communities of primary relationships are systems that define the constraints and possibilities for certain kinds of experiences. The nature of these experiences is unique to each particular system in relation to its own story and social location. For example, a family with elementary children is a system that has evolved certain patterns of relating over a number of years within extended families with their own expectations and within a culture with its values and language. The possibilities for meaning for this family are a direct result of its history and its social location, as well as the interaction of the persons who make up the family.

(3) *Larger Social Systems*

Into this category of community belong many types of systems that involve some interaction and have more or less influence on the life of persons. Examples are neighborhoods, villages, cities, states, nations, ethnic and reference groups, gender, economic class, international relations, global ecology, and many more. One can conceive of life in terms of overlapping and interdependent communities which compete and cooperate in many ways for the benefit and/or detriment of the few or the many. Each level of community can be analyzed in terms of its subgroups, its unique dynamics, and its relations with other communities.

In modern, urban life, persons participate actively in and are decisively influenced by many communities. Such participation and influence are most obvious during times of crisis, such as an economy failing to provide adequate living for its citizens, or international conflict that leads to war, or global pollution that threatens the health of all. But even when particular communities function appropriately, their influence is important because they define certain possibilities and constraints for human experience. Each community has its own history which defines its life, and its particular social location which defines its relation to other communities.

(4) *God*

God is a word often used to refer to the most universal community that one can imagine. The conception of God varies, depending on the experiences and imagination of particular traditions, and it is always mysterious because it points to a level of community about which our understanding is cloudy. Christians tend to believe that God is personal and active and loving as well as universal, and point to biblical stories to illustrate these qualities of God's character. God as the creator and sustainer of all things means that God's perspective includes every perspective in the universe and thereby unifies these perspectives into a totality that transcends every other perspective. That God became human in Jesus Christ and was revealed as a God of love means that God is involved in intimate interaction with all creatures to bring them into harmony with all that is.

There is a sense in which God is the most distant perspective from the individual person because of God's universal character. At the same time, God is the most intimate of partners because God is active at the center of human becoming. Theology refers to this dual locus of God as transcendence and immanence. God is the perspective on all the communities of the world and so transcends the reality of any particular community. As such, God is a perspective which no community can grasp. God works to increase value in the world by influence on the decisions of communities. Thus God is immanent in the concreteness of all life.

It is appropriate to conceptualize God as a community, the universal community of all things. But the biblical witness is to a God that is not only universal (the perspective on everything that is), but God who is also personal and loving and interacts with the creation. Charles Hartshorne imagined God as analogous to the human person—a complex society of societies, but with a center of consciousness that coordinates the body and its actions. Likewise, God can be imagined as the community of all communities but with a center of consciousness that interacts with the world with love and purpose.[11]

Given this analogy for God as community, we can see that God has a history. God's history is in part the history of the world, that is, the development and interaction of the many communities that make up the creation. It is a confession of faith to say that God's character has been decisively revealed in certain historical events, such as the Exodus and the life and death of Jesus. But every community with a belief in God points to some narrative as revealing the presence of God. Communities are sustained as they remember their stories and reinterpret their meaning for the present. For each community of faith, God has a story which is told and retold as a way of connecting the particular identity to a sense of the universal and ultimate life of God.

Likewise, God has a socio-political context. That context is the uniqueness and integrity of the many communities that make up the world. Creating a world of harmony and adventure that moves toward beauty requires some coordination of the nearly infinite number of centers of freedom in the world. Thus, part of the social context for God is the socio-political matrix of the communities of the world but viewed from a perspective that is possible only for God. The religous task for the faithful is to see the world as God sees it. This is both impossible and necessary, for God is the only one with the perspective and the unwavering love to see the world as it is and to envision its real possibilities for the future. Yet, the essence of faith is to become partners with God in sustaining and redeeming the world.

The Socio-political Context

Each moment of community life has a socio-political context. That is, no community lives in isolation to itself with only its own story forming its identity. Rather, every moment of community life includes its relationships with many other communities. Some are subgroups within the community, such as families within a congregation. Such subgroups respond partly to the larger community of the congregation and partly to its many relationships with other communities. Some communities are parallel, such as other congregations, other charity and civic groups, and many others. Some communities are larger and more inclusive: local, state, and national governments, business and industry, international organizations. Every particular community, such as a congregation, finds itself within a web of relationships[12] which help determine the possibilities and constraints.

One of the characteristics of the socio-political context of community is that its full scope is not readily apparent. Each community tends to foster its own self-interest in ways that benefit some parts of the larger community more than others. The biblical prophets constantly pointed to the poor and disenfranchised who tended to be overlooked in the politics between communities. Modern liberation theologies are trying to help us envision the relationship between all communities. Because all human life is part of the one global community, all are interdependent. The consequences of decisions in one part of the global community have a direct impact on the possibilities of other parts. When decisions are made without regard for this interdependence, the consequences can be devastating: nuclear danger, hunger, political instability.

There is a risk in every discussion of community of overlooking or underestimating the significance of the historical and socio-political context of community life. There is an idolatry of community that focuses only on the internal dynamics and makes of consensus a god which does not take into account the historical identity of the community and its movement toward universal values, or which does not sensitize itself to the radical political nature of relationships between communities. Every moment is a moment in an ongoing story, and results in actions which have far-reaching effects on other communities near and far.

When Mary Archer challenged her congregation to be more faithful to their Christian identity by becoming more active in a deteriorating urban community, she was taking seriously the historical and socio-political context of their shared life. From such a combination came new life and power. But such openness to the past and the present context also involved a risk to chaos that required balance and artistic response. But only such risk avoids the idolatry of community which is tempting but deadly.

The *Bible* shows the roots of a radical prophecy, which can challenge the rich and lead the poor from their oppression. Prophecy is born by a radical reinterpretation of one's own story, and by a radical openness to the other communities which form the context of one's life.[13] When such a radical prophetic tradition is alive and active within a particular community, life may not

137

be stable and comfortable, but it is more likely to be faithful to the one God of communion and adventure.

We have identified several characteristics of loving community. It is a process of interaction which is dynamic. It occurs within a historical and socio-political context which must be taken with utmost seriousness in order to have a built-in self-critique that prevents idolatry. Now, we turn to the images of value that help determine the direction in which community life is moving. A loving community is one which is moving toward creativity, justice, intimacy, and faith. We will examine each of these constructs as symbols of the internal dynamics of community life.

Creativity

Every community develops shared patterns of behavior. Whenever a sequence of behavior becomes actual, it is likely to be reproduced. When a particular sequence becomes established as a regular and expected pattern, it becomes a rule, a habit, a ritual. Such patterns are necessary for community life to exist, and they provide the basis of significant symbols in communication. However, every pattern tends to become rigid, habitual, routinized, and thus unresponsive to the changing needs of the community members and the larger context. Creativity as a value is interaction that fosters a balance of continuity and change so as to preserve the necessary patterns and encourage maximum flexibility in the future.[14]

For example, the Terrytown congregation had engaged in a standard form of evangelistic service for many years. They felt obligated to engage in evangelism, and knew only the pattern they had inherited, even though it did not meet the needs of the members or provide opportunities for new people to discover their community. A pattern of behavior which had probably served the congregation well in the past was continued out of habit without regard for its effectiveness within the present context. As a result, there was a lack of energy involved in these habits, and the emphasis on evangelism itself was in danger, in spite of the sense of obligation to do something.

Creativity is essentially the restoration of flexible patterns of behavior to replace behaviors which have become rigid and narrow and ineffective. In this case, the pastor and congregation began to look for new forms of evangelism which would preserve their commitment to sharing the gospel with new persons, but in new patterns of behavior that were more appropriate for the congregation and the local community. Their study led them to design a plan of hospitality evangelism which replaced the evangelistic meetings and drew on the new energies and vision of the people. The final result was new creativity for this community.

The Scriptures consistently point to God's invitation to creativity. Abraham was called to leave his familiar land to risk his future in an unknown territory. God's people were frequently called to risk their familiar patterns and trust in the God of the future. Yet the Scriptures also testify that the vision of the new possibilities, the new creation that God is doing, is continuous with the past. The transition from old and familiar to the new often feels discontinuous, but the seeds of the change are already present in the past. Therefore, the virtue of creativity involves both a deeper sensitivity to the past as well as a radical trust in new and untried possibilities.[15] A ministry of creativity will support the rituals and habits that form the basis of dependable community life, but it will also be sensitive to the tendency to rigid patterns that is present in every community, and encourage new possibilities that more effectively meet the needs of the members and the changing demands and challenges from the larger communities.

Justice

Shared patterns of behavior in community life take the form of social structures that determine the boundaries of the community (who participates and who does not participate in which activities) and the distribution of power (who leads and who follows). In order to endure over time, a community must have a structure that is both stable and flexible. It must be able to withstand the entrance and exit of members from the community and be able to prevent intrusion from outside when necessary. It must be flexible to allow basic changes in leadership and membership when this change is necessary. Rules on boundaries and leadership must be clear, stable, and open to revision in order to keep a community vital.[16]

Justice as a value is interaction that fosters mutuality in social structure so that persons have access to resources for meaningful life and participation in defining the character of their communities. A just community encourages participation in decision-making at levels appropriate to the task at hand and to the maturity of its members. A just community calls out leadership that can be effective and also responsive to the whole community within its historical and socio-political context.

For example, at Trinity Lutheran Church, the congregation tended to view the pastor as the minister for the church and to view laypersons as passive participants. But Pastor Linter became convinced that Martin Luther had a vision of a more active laity. What had become a structure of the overburdened pastor and the underused laity seemed to Pastor Linter as untrue to the best of their own history. If such a social structure were continued, it would be an issue of justice; persons were not being challenged by their community to participate fully in the community, especially to its marginal members, the sick and shut-ins.

So the pastor called, trained, and sent out a group of deacons as pastoral assistants. The change involved some threat, because the pastor had to share leadership in a new way, the laypersons had to risk involvement with others, and the marginal members had to accept visits from someone other than the pastor. But Bible study and continuous interpretation made the changes possible, and the community moved toward greater justice.

The Bible points to justice as a part of God's nature. Through the prophets, God made known the impor- tance of the marginal and peripheral persons (widows and orphans), the foreigner, even enemies. The prophetic tradition, including Jesus, calls the commu- nity leadership to greater sensitivity to the needs of all people. The communities are condemned that ignore the claims of the weak and that tolerate leadership that is narrowly self-serving. All persons are invited to dine at God's table where the leaders are the servants of all and justice is the mark of faithfulness.

The virtue of justice in community moves toward a full mutuality in which every member participates in ways that are appropriate and beneficial for all. A ministry of justice pays close attention to issues of boundaries and leadership. Just boundaries fairly determine the membership of a community in its various activities so the community can function effectively without being unduly exclusive. Just leadership is sensitive to the needs of the community within the socio-political context and can act with courage to engage the community in its joint work with God.

Intimacy

Community life involves shared patterns of interaction and shared social structures. Community life also involves shared emotional bonding and loyalty which provides occasions for intimacy. A loving community is one that fosters a balance of emotional closeness and individual autonomy so as to enhance the loyalty that supports the corporate fabric as well as the growth in maturity of its members.[17]

Communities apparently vary in their ability to provide images and occasions for intimacy to develop. Communities with rigid and authoritarian patterns will inhibit the development of maturity necessary for true intimacy. Communities that are chaotic and permissive will not foster the engagement of persons that facilitate intimacy. Finding the appropriate balance between engaged sensitivity to others and encouragement of autonomous development is difficult. The ability to join with others in cooperative endeavors and yet be able to tolerate ambiguity and frustration is a sign of maturity.

A community of intimacy is one in which the different levels of maturity will be taken into account. Those in the early stages of development, in formation, need secure and dependable relationships and a relatively homogeneous world view. Those in the testing periods of their development need a plurality of images of meaning and flexible authority figures who can encourage and limit behavioral experimentation until new levels of maturity and responsibility are reached. Those in the various stages of maturity need challenging opportunities for further growth and younger generations to care for.

Loss of rhythm and balance in one's emotional attachments is frequent for persons and communities. When such loss of intimacy occurs, life becomes routine, technical, and alienating. Without appropriate intimacy, the human spirit experiences loneliness and isolation and the result is often a life of emptiness and resentment. A loving community fosters intimacy by being sensitive to the many levels of bonding and attachment that occur within and beyond the community boundaries, and by encouraging deep sharing that enables the human spirit at its fragile center to be nurtured.

Because of his training in Clinical Pastoral Education, Pastor Brown was especially sensitive to the emotional needs of his people. When he began training a small group in lay ministry of visitation to the aging and sick, he focused not only on the needs of the persons being visited, but also on the experiences of the visitors. He discovered that their ability to minister was directly related to their own emotional maturity and their ability to be intimate with those who were lonely, angry, and discouraged. As the visitors came to understand themselves better and share deeply their own issues with one another, their effectiveness in ministry improved, and their satisfaction increased. Both the lay visitors and those visited had experiences of intimacy that contributed to individual growth and community enrichment.

Intimacy between God and God's people, and intimacy within the community of faith, is an important theme of the Scriptures. The first person was lonely until a partner was created that met the deepest needs for companionship. High points in the Bible are the theophanies with God's people: Moses at the burning bush and on Mt. Sinai, Elijah in the cave, the psalmist in prayer, Jesus in Gethsemane, the Apostles at Pentecost. At the Last Supper, Jesus washed the disciples' feet as a symbol of their unity and common loyalty. The ritual of bread and cup is the symbol of intimate communion for the church. The virtue of intimacy within community points to the deep needs of persons for emotional bonding and attachments that are appropriate to their personal needs and to the context of the interaction. A community that is moving toward intimacy will foster occasions for deep sharing and the development of loyalties, as well as seek a rhythm with the need for personal identity and autonomy.

Faith

Shared meaning is a product of the available images and stories of a particular community and its tradition. Human perception itself is made possible by language which discloses and hides the various aspects of full experience. Experiences for which there are rich and powerful images will have deep significance for the community. Experiences for which there is no language will be ignored and considered mysterious. Language determines the horizons of meaning that are available to a particular people.

Religion is sometimes defined as the interpretation of experience at the boundary of language and the mystery it cannot disclose. The images of meaning contained in language will be clues about the perception of reality that is allowed and encouraged in a community with its particular strengths and limitations.[18] The virtue of faith is the movement toward larger and deeper images and language so that the full richness of experience is available to a community. The tension within this virtue occurs in the balance between commitment to particular images that can provide depth of understanding and commitment and openness to new images of life and transformation. Difficulty occurs within communities when images of reality and ultimacy are inadequate for the shared experiences and interaction with other communities. A ministry that facilitates movement

144

toward faith will help a community identify the images that have power and also lead them to be critical of their images and to be open to larger perspectives on reality.

The Prince of Peace Church was one that had its images of meaning challenged by its changing socio-political context. Its successful past was ended when urban change brought in a population of poor, black families. Its attempts to adjust to the new situation did not work at first. But they held on to a vision of community of faith that is open to all persons and that follows a God of universal love.

The meaning of this image was challenged by the clash of culture, social and economic class. However, their deepened image of God who calls them to welcome all into the household of God, and to welcome strangers in the name of Christ, enabled them to risk radical changes in social structure and leadership until they had discovered a new way of being that was relevant to the new challenges. This was a community whose images of meaning moved toward a more universal faith in a loving God of all people.

Summary

Our goal in this chapter has been to explore the metaphor of community formation as a basis for ministry. We have focused on the local community of faith as our primary illustration. Community is an ambiguous symbol for ministry because it represents both the idealized hopes of persons for true belonging and because it often reminds us of our disappointments and loneliness. We have tried to describe the nature of community so that it has enough breadth and complexity to account for the many levels of human experience in its depth and ambiguity. Earlier, we suggested a fairly simple definition that focused on the virtues of loving community. Now, we suggest a more complex definition:

Loving community is a process of interaction within a historical and socio-political context characterized by:
—shared patterns of interaction that move toward creativity
—shared social structures that move toward justice
—shared loyalties that move toward intimacy and
—shared meanings that move toward faith

If community formation is an adequate metaphor for ministry, its usefulness will have to be tested at many levels of religious and secular life. We turn now to a discussion of education for professional ministry within the theological schools and seminaries to further test our ideas.

The Challenge
to Ministry Education

In a previous chapter we saw that ministry as community formation includes establishing a covenant, critical awareness of the situation, critical awareness of the tradition, focused community planning, and reinterpreting the interplay of covenant and tradition. The designated pastor relates so as to encourage and stimulate the formation of community. The pastor finds a role that stands between the interpretive and political processes in a way that gives expression to the unique style and abilities of the pastor. We have seen the pastor's role as midwife to community formation in various traditions and various situations. In this chapter, we address the question of ministerial education for such a ministerial role.

Commentators on modern seminary education in the Western world are saying that contemporary ministerial training has many severe problems.[1] Seminary education is fragmented into various subject areas which have become isolated as specialties. Bible, church history, theology, and the various practical disciplines have developed unique methodologies and have become increasingly specialized. Furthermore, the various disciplines have sub-disciplines that represent further specialization. In biblical studies one finds form criticism, redaction criticism, and canon criticism, to name a few. Theology is divided into fundamental theology, kerygmatic theology, apologetic theology, and others. The process of specialization continues seemingly without limit. In their separate disciplines and professional organizations, proponents of such disciplines find it difficult to be in touch with one another.

Furthermore, the specializations are dictated by secular methodologies rather than theological or ecclesial considerations. The various specialized methodologies do not in themselves enhance the sense of the holy. For example, biblical studies take their methodology from modern forms of historical and literary criticism. Such criticism can identify probable causes and relationships, but additional knowledge in no way guarantees greater faith. Pastoral care is led by secular counseling methodologies, but these in no way assure a greater sense of devotion to God. All across the seminary curriculum the various methodologies presume faith, but in no way do they give assurance that faith will be enhanced.

Another criticism is that the seminary curriculum is not related enough to congregational life. The result is that seminary students find their ecclesial ties and relationships weakened rather than strengthened by the experience of seminary education. The natural process whereby congregations recognize and respond to those with great gifts of faithful leadership and discernment is broken by seminary education. Graduates often take five years or more to establish ecclesial relationships wherein natural gifts of faithfulness can be recognized. The seminary sources of scholarship frequently remain cut off from the church, kept within an educational elite that is very far removed from most people in local congregations.

Yet another criticism is that seminary education

remains abstract and verbal. Seminary graduates are schooled in many theories and ideas, but are peculiarly inept in relating to congregations. Since ministry cannot be practiced in an isolated school setting, graduates come away relatively unpracticed in ministry.

A criticism that moves in the opposite direction is that seminary education is not thoughtful enough. Seminaries are too much influenced by fads in theology, specializing in whatever movement is popular at the time, whether it be death of God, liberation, or church growth. Seminaries are too caught up in a proliferation of pactical courses. Churches expect every concern to be represented in the seminary curriculum, and pressure is put upon the seminaries. Stewardship, counseling, evangelism, feminist concerns, preaching, worship, marriage enrichment, peace education, political action, journalism, finance, urbanism, group process, mass media, moral development, and many more are pushed upon the seminaries. Seminaries are so responsive to these various movements that they lose the capacity to be profoundly thoughtful. Action and reflection methodologies encourage instant theologizing, quick responses to whatever is offered. The disciplines of scholarship are replaced by agility of response.

Still another criticism is that seminaries are in bondage to upper middle-class interest, male interest for the most part. While a third or more of the students are women in many seminaries, few faculty members are women. The concerns of blacks, Hispanics, and Native Americans also go begging. The concerns of Asian and African Christians are seldom represented. Therefore, seminaries serve to perpetuate rather narrow upper middle-class interests.

Perhaps this list is sufficient to suggest that seminary education is being powerfully criticized for being too fragmented, unrelated to actual life issues, overly

149

abstract, too subject to theological fads, and not responsive to minority interests. In our judgment, many of the problems of seminary education stem from the tendency of such education to lose touch with ministry as community formation. The basic teaching reality of the seminary is the actual experience of community formation to be found there. When the seminary classes and other experiences focus principally on an abstracted version of life outside the seminary, then the living covenant within the seminary and the process of interpretation become detached from each other. The covenant shaping, celebrative, and interpreted experience of seminary life within its wider community context is the principal teaching resource of the seminary.

A seminary is a community of faith. It is not a congregation in one sense because its students come for only a brief time and have a special vocation of study rather than the wider range of congregational commitments. However, in another sense seminary communities are like congregations; covenantal relationships and ecclesial significance undergird seminary life. Every class can become an exercise in the enrichment of the formation of community. Biblical study, theology, and pastoral care have immediate relevance to all the people at hand. Worship, student affairs, and faculty selection have direct and fundamental impact upon the relationships within the community. To spend years ignoring, becoming detached from, and turning away from such community-forming relationships makes students less able rather than more able to minister.

Theological training is properly done within the setting of community formation. The study of theology is properly a covenant-enriching activity. When the seminary considers itself to be primarily an academy where the faculty and students reflect about the church's nature and function beyond themselves, then the students learn to take a stance of detachment that is disengaged from the actual living relationships of the church. The seminary can study theology seriously only to the degree that it takes its own community processes seriously and to the degree that it understands these processes within the larger community contexts in the church and in the world.[2]

A seminary's primary resource for study and reflection is the body of lives and relationships between the persons who are its membership. The ongoing historical study of the Scriptures and the church is set within the community context of the seminary. Decisions about worship, study, and field education are theological questions. Decisions about vocation, direction of study, and family problems are similarly theological questions. Seminary decisions about curriculum, admissions, credit, graduation, development, and finance are all theological questions. They are the same kind of questions that every congregation must face, even though they may differ in detail. A seminary has a natural set of relationships with its sponsoring churches, other seminaries, and various public institutions. These natural relationships are part of the wider community setting of the school. The decisions about which institutions, which relationships, and what should be done involve deeply theological questions. Community formation takes place around just such issues. Focusing upon these relationships for reflection is the proper practical theology of seminary education.

Clinical education, ministry in hospitals, and field work assignments in churches usually include theological reflection upon actual cases according to an action/reflection model. When this is done without consideration of the present living relationships and of the institutional setting, then the whole process may seem detached and abstract. The relationships between

151

a seminary and supporting congregations are very worthy of reflection by students and faculty. Decisions about such relationships are analogous to the relationships between a congregation and its supporting institutions. To learn to think about supporting relationships within a seminary enables students to think concretely about the actual supporting relationships of a congregation. To focus on community formation in the training institution enables students to focus on community formation in congregations to which they will later minister.

Such considerations would suggest that the field education committee ought to include student and faculty voices. Field education decisions should be thought of as questions of faithfulness, i.e., as theological questions. When the committee asks that cooperating congregations furnish students with a variety of ministry experiences and that local pastors meet with their students weekly, the committee is making a request that should be considered in terms of both the congregation's mission and the seminary's mission. Such questions are deeply theological questions. If the committee cannot see them as theological questions, no doubt students in the field education program will seldom be able to locate the theological issues in local church administration.

Another way of making the same point is to say that seminary communities should let their actual praxis be the subject of joint reflection. While students are in training for ministry, the seminary context shapes their praxis. Study traditionally takes the form of analyzing problems beyond the classroom. Ideas may thereby be changed, but in separation from lived praxis. The separation of theory and practice is enlarged. When the dominant community patterns as lived become the subject of discussion, study, and decision, a shared praxis develops.[3] A step toward the healing of the separation of theory and practice is taken. To move toward reflection upon living praxis is to prepare to minister in other settings.

We have been insisting that when community formation is taken as a primary goal of ministry, then training for ministry will focus on community formation. Furthermore, the focus on community formation in the training setting will not be simply an abstract consideration of principles, but will engage students and faculty in the community formation processes of the school's life and mission. This means that the relationships, covenants, and institutional affiliations become the subject of faculty and student interpretation. Lest such reflection become too introverted, it must always be seen within the larger mission of the school, the supporting institutions, and the individual students. For students to become adept at care, politics, and interpretation of their own relationships to a particular institution equips them to relate in similar ways with other institutions. In this way, the breach between seminary and congregation can be at least partially healed.

Suppose the reader grants that community formation is an appropriate goal of ministry and suppose the reader further grants that students may gain skills in community formation by attending to the actual relationships within the theological school. The reader may then ask whether such a perspective makes any actual difference in seminary education. What difference will it make in curriculum, teaching, student life, and faculty responsibilities? The curriculum of most seminaries is now divided into four parts: Bible, church history, theology/ethics, and the practical disciplines (such as counseling, preaching, worship, administration, education, evangelism). Though faculty constantly ask students to integrate the subjects, integration is seldom done well.

Students could have a series of classes in which the focus is not on a traditional discipline, but on the student's vocation, the relationships among students, issues of student life, seminary administrative questions, the relationship of seminary and other institutions. The intersection of the seminary's mission and the student's vocation would become the primary focus. This particular focus is related to the larger question of the church's mission in the world. All is related to God's will and purpose for these particular persons within the context of these institutions and their missions.

Such classes would focus on the underlying and very practical questions of community formation. They require careful exegetical study of Scripture, church history, and denominational tradition. They also require careful theological and ethical study. Since the questions are related to actual decisions to be made, they certainly involve the practical disciplines. Such processes should help make the students and the institution more whole because the underlying and pressing questions of living and survival are not set aside. They become the very content for theological consideration.

For example, one seminary class took as a major topic of study the interracial conflict occurring in the immediate neighborhood. Instances of actual open conflict between the races in the surrounding area became the focus of discussion. In some cases, students had been confronted directly by interracial violence, and the question in class became one of how to react in those situations. However, the class also discussed the influence of the seminary in the neighborhood. What power did the seminary have to change the situation? How much energy should be devoted to such a question when the primary task of the seminary is study of the tradition? These were lively disussions, and they involved in a very practical way the questions of community formation.

The immediate implication for seminary curriculum is that considerable credit must be allowed for courses that deal with community-formation issues. The most innovative curriculum changes of recent years have been in the direction of wider cultural analysis and the interfacing of the biblical/historical tradition with the results of the wider cultural analysis.[4] Courses then tend to move through the cycle of cultural analysis, traditional studies, missional studies. This threefold curriculum replaces the older curriculum of Bible, history, theology, and practice. Our suggestion moves toward cultural analysis. However, the newer threefold curriculum can have the same difficulties as the older one had. The threefold curriculum may also be abstract, detached, and unrelated to student concerns. Graduates may still be weak in their abilities to engage congregations in ministry.

Whether within the older fourfold, or the newer threefold curriculum, students and faculty together need the occasion to address actual questions and relationships that constitute their being together. Cultural analysis may contribute substantially to a better understanding of the dynamics of the relationships between persons within the theological school, of the sense of vocation, and of the institutional mission. However, the cultural analysis must become located in those relationships if it is to become a practical ministering skill for students.

The focus on community formation means that the curriculum must give way to a heavy focus on questions of community relationships and interpretation. The important clue is not so much whether a fourfold traditional curriculum is followed, or whether a threefold revised curriculum is followed. The clue is, rather, the extent to which course time is given to the underlying and immediate questions of community formation. If serious attention is given to problems of student life, wider cultural questions as they press upon the community, and relationships to other institutions, then the content of traditional courses will inevitably begin to change. Biblical exegesis will address immediate community questions. Historical study will attempt to set more immediate community questions within their larger and more classical context. Preaching and worship will be addressed to students confronted with exams. Questions of pastoral care will involve other students and faculty in the classroom. The focus on community formation becomes a basis for either the threefold or fourfold curriculum.

Perhaps it seems that the practical disciplines have swallowed the disciplines of exegesis, history, and theology. Such is not the case. Rather, the effort is to let the traditional disciplines become located. Courses in community formation are to be rigorously exegetical and self-consciously historical. Community formation courses are to engage in disciplines of theological and ethical analysis. They are to be concerned about care of one another and about the mission of the school. If community formation falls into mere exchange of opinion, then it will have gained concreteness at the cost of disciplined analysis and reflection. The traditional disciplines should flourish rather than atrophy. What is gained by the students is skill in relating traditional disciplines to the immediate situation.

Community formation courses can fall into the trap of becoming merely instant theology. The student and faculty determination to maintain quality can stand against triviality. The method of practical theology as described earlier in this book indicates the various elements in a serious discussion. According to that method, there must be a serious description of some actual event, some actual praxis. This can be in the form of a verbatim, a case, or an autobiographical account. Then the method moves to a disciplined analysis of the event, thereby opening out the various dimensions of the situation.

The method moves to a study of Scripture, history, and theology. The study of the tradition for any given event could well become a discipline for many months or years. Faculty and students together can decide how far to pursue analogies in Scripture, church history, theology, and ethics. The study of the tradition is a basic and fundamental moment in the class. If traditional studies of Scripture, history, and theology are not strong, then the whole process becomes weak.

Out of the critical study of the event and of the analogies in the tradition comes a normative convictional evaluation of the event. The event is re-narrated in terms of the study and discussion. The narrative is challenged for systematic bias. The narrative sets the framework for discussion of particular principles of action. If students and faculty challenge one another honestly regarding such study and discussion, then the quality of scholarship can be maintained without losing touch with the formation of community.

The quality of traditional disciplines is kept high by professional groups that set standards. Old and New Testament studies have professional groups. So do historical, theological, and practical disciplines. These professional groups of faculty specialists meet together, publish materials, and generally set the requirements for the quality of the field. In the case of community formation, the specialists are the members of the community. Representative students and faculty meeting together should publish materials and generally set the requirements for quality in the community formation classes. As in all classes, the responsibility for quality is finally jointly shared.

Edward Farley has argued that seminary curricula lack the *habitus* of theology.[5] He seems to mean that every person of faith is constantly searching out God's will. Such a search for God's will is immediately related to personal faith and to the study of Scripture. Theology as habitus is personal, self-engaging, and constantly active. Formal theological study has made of theology an object of study, a matter of knowing the history of the arguments and issues. Objective knowledge about theology has replaced the personal, self-engaging search for God's will that goes on in the life of every faithful person.

We consider that a focus on ministry for community formation is supportive of Farley's suggestion. Since the object of community formation is immediate life issues, actual relationships, genuine questions of vocation and mission, they are the particular expressions of the search for God's will individually and communally. Whereas theological study often tends to objectify theological questions, as Farley indicates, classes in community formation are intended to carry out study, discussion, and dialogue about God's will for us now in relation to the issues being presented. The pressing questions and serious doubts of students regarding their own faith are the most appropriate material for community formation. The issues need not be framed only in an individual way. The search for direction in this class, in this school, in this denomination, and in this nation is intensely appropriate. Surely, these communal questions are an exercise of theology as *habitus*.

Should one not speak, then, of "spiritual formation" rather than community formation? Indeed, one could speak of spiritual formation. However, the term "spiritual formation" has its own history, one that is heavily related to the relationship between a spiritual director and an advisee. We are suggesting, rather, that a group of students and faculty together address the fundamental relationships and issues that constitute their life and mission together, and that they pursue these questions to the root question of God's will for them individually, together, and as a part of a much larger community and world. Such a process does not conform to traditional spiritual formation, even though it is without question a kind of spiritual formation. However, we believe that the term "community formation" comes closer to describing what we intend.

A community formation curriculum challenges traditional relationships between students and faculty in a very fundamental way. Traditional faculty are masters of the disciplines, and they require the students to learn the subject matter of those disciplines. The primary mode of learning is lecture, study, writing, and discussion, with faculty deciding when the result is qualitatively acceptable. A community formation curriculum understands faculty and students to be mutually engaged in a process together. The exchange between student and faculty is basic to the community process. The goal of education is for students and faculty to become equally members of a committed community. The student voice at all levels of community reflection is therefore essential. For example, the student voice is a part of the selection of a new faculty member. Such student participation at all levels of communty is enormously educative for the students. It breaks the separation between theory and practice, between tradition and decision, between the study of theology and the practice of ministry. It will require considerable adjustment in the attitudes of both students and faculty, but that is exactly what we need.[6]

The Doctor of Ministry

In recent years, many seminaries have begun to offer a Doctor of Ministry degree. The most prevalent D.Min. degree is an in-service degree, which means that the student is an active pastor who carries out his or her study while continuing in the pastorate. Doctor of Ministry degrees are set up to enhance the skill of the pastor while the pastor continues to minister. A variety of specialized D.Min. degrees has been created, from pastoral care, stewardship, and family ministry to administration. However, most D.Min. degrees aim at the general improvement of pastoral skills.

The Doctor of Ministry degree has introduced a whole set of problems of its own.[7] It can have the effect of pulling the pastor away from the congregation because of the special study and on-campus experiences required. The D.Min. can become the special concern of only one or two faculty members on campus, while other faculty needs are filled by employing adjunct persons. Standards may vary greatly from one D.Min. program to another.[8] Many D.Min. programs feature specialization in research and research methods, something that has little direct benefit for the congregation. While the D.Min. may have the effect of drawing seminaries closer to congregational life, there are many inherent difficulties.

Since, in our view, ministry should aim principally at community formation and interpretation, a Doctor of Ministry degree is properly a degree in community formation and interpretation. The various specializations mentioned above have an important place in the conception of community formation. Therefore, the degree can be carried out in a variety of ways.

We suggest that the D.Min. curriculum should begin with a covenant building process. The covenant is not simply between faculty and students. Rather, the covenant is also between student and student, and between student and congregation. The concrete study of community formation engages the community in which one is located. A pastor studying community formation will examine the relationships within the congregation where he or she is pastor. The program should be of benefit to the congregation as well as to the pastor. It is difficult to imagine improving pastoral skills without a direct benefit to the congregation. If a pastor becomes more adept at the study of the Book of Amos, but the congregation is unaffected by it, then the pastor hardly deserves a degree in ministry. To initiate a D.Min. program, the pastor negotiates a covenant with the congregation as well as with the other students and with the seminary faculty.

A student entering a D.Min. program already has an ongoing covenant with a congregation or some other church-related institution. To enter the D.Min. program will require some adjustment in that ongoing covenant. Very specifically, the conregation and the pastor must make allowance for the additional study required by the program. The pastor's schedule must be rearranged, and the pastor and congregation will have to find ways in which the various pastoral activities continue to be cared for. The pastor will have to consider where she or he is vocationally and what particular skills need additional training. However, the congregation can very well have a voice in helping assess what skills need additional training. In a word, application to a Doctor of Ministry program raises probing questions about the covenant between the congregation and the pastor. Those very questions can become the subject matter for study and consideration in the program itself.

The covenant between students and faculty can easily fall into a traditional pattern of faculty as the removed, but knowledgeable, experts and the students as energetic, but largely uncritical, recipients. However, when the relationships among students and faculty become a matter for consideration and reflection, then the community formational basis of ministry comes to the fore. Faculty become learners with students, and students help establish standards for one another. Such a consideration does not obliterate the legitimate expertise of faculty, but it does elevate the legitimate expertise of students. Nor does such a consideration rule out traditional modes of teaching, e.g., lecturing. It does, however, mean that teaching methods must include much attention to mutual criticism and reflection. Student voices and considerations become highly important in arriving at standards of acceptable performance. One can hardly teach students the skills of community formation in the local congregation without attending to those same skills in the academic process.

After having established or revised a covenant with the congregation, and after having established a covenant with other students and faculty, the student is ready to begin the process of in-service training. The educational key to in-service training for ministry is the creation of limited in-service ministry events. The limited ministry events stand within the ongoing congregational purposes. If they are to attribute to community formation, then they must fit into the community's self-understanding and ongoing story. They must also be the occasion for the exercise of ongoing pastoral leadership. If "ministry events" do not get into the various relationships and routines of the congregational life, then they can hardly be community forming. It is, of course, easy for a pastor to carve out a reading project that may have much scholarly merit but has no relevance to the congregational life. Such a reading project may be very worthy as a scholarly exercise, but it can hardly be worthy as a ministry event unless the scholarship is related to the life of the congregation. The point is that there are many ways to allow a so-called "ministry event" to turn into a "non-ministry event." There are many ways that a D.Min. ministry activity can actually pull a student away from community formation.

What has just been said must be qualified in several ways. Genuine and worthy relationship to the ongoing life of a congregation requires the best scholarship that a pastor can muster. The above comments are not to be interpreted as a criticism of scholarship for pastoral ministry. Such scholarship is very much needed, and it should certainly be a central part of a Doctor of Ministry program. Another qualification is that the effects of scholarship are not always immediately evident. Sometimes the community-forming power of scholarship may show up some time later, perhaps years later.

Nevertheless, since a D.Min. program aims at improvement in ministerial ability, in our judgment the program should aim at community formation and interpretation, as those terms have been developed in this book. Appropriately, a D.Min. limited ministry event is one in which scholarship has some direct bearing to interrelationships and self-understanding within a congregation. The ministry event has to do with the living relationships by which the nurture and mission of a congregation are carried out.

Limited ministry events should, therefore, have two sets of objectives. They should be set within the community-forming processes of the congregation. Some limited statement of purpose regarding community formation within that congregation ought to be primary in the ministry event. The purpose might be as limited as improved staff communication, or attention to several neglected persons. The purpose may be as large as greater participation of all members of the congregation, or as the development of new ecumenical relationships. The possibilities are endless. Nevertheless, a ministry event rests upon engagement in some more limited community-forming process.

If a ministry event includes, first of all, a limited objective of community formation and interpretation, it must also include an objective regarding the pastoral role. The second objective of a ministry event, therefore, concerns what must be learned within the pastoral role if the community-formational objective is to be carried out. If the community formation requires no pastoral leadership, though it be worthy enough in its own right, it can hardly be appropriate as a pastoral ministry event.

Suppose a pastor decides that a ministry event is to focus on the healing effect of preaching in the congregation. Furthermore, suppose that a representative body of the congregation encourages the pastor's concern about preaching. They decide that members of an evaluation group will carry out several conversations each week with persons who have heard the preaching. The evaluation group and the pastor are then to assess the effect of the preaching on those who are being interviewed each week. The community-formational objective has been established.

The student must then focus equal attention on the pastoral role. What constitutes preaching for healing? The student and faculty may decide upon a reading list drawn from the biblical and theological literature about healing. The student may also want to study literature on preaching. The student might furthermore want to tape the sermons in order to be able to replay them. Perhaps the evaluation group would listen to the recorded sermons, trying to find relationships to what was reported by their interviewees. There are myriad possibilities. Yet, in each case, the student attempts to set up an intentional direction in the ministerial role that corresponds to the intended goal in community formation.

More generally stated, the pastor's role is one of discerning, encouraging, interpreting, giving direction to, and being responsive to tendencies toward community formation. The opposite tendencies are always present, e.g., tendencies to isolation, alienation, segregation, malevolence, and disruptive conflict. Not that conflict is always disruptive. Conflict can be the energy for community-forming vitality, but conflict can also become disruptive. The pastor works toward the renewal and enrichment of community. Therefore, community-forming goals always give rise to corresponding goals for ministerial practice. Since goal language is very much oriented to achievement, it must be set within the larger and more fundamental process that is interpreted as God's grace and ongoing providence. The community being formed is the community of God's will, and the ministry being enacted is a service of gratitude in response to God's marvelous grace. The process of worship and interpreting God's grace and love become the most central community-forming events. The pastoral role of leading worship and interpreting Scripture thereby corresponds in a fundamental way to the formation of community.

We have said that limited in-service ministry events stand within the ongoing congregational story. They include a twofold objective: one for community formation and another for the pastoral role corresponding to the community-formation objective. It follows that the limited ministry event must engage appropriate groups and persons within the congregation. In the example above, the pastor worked with a representative body in agreeing to the event, with the evaluation group, and the evaluation group was, in turn, to work with interviewees. All of these persons are appropriate to a vision of preaching as congregational healing.

We have stated frequently that the ministry event is a part of the congregation's ongoing story. This means that the ministry event is set within an ongoing interpretive process. In our example, the congregation must decide whether to accept a focus on healing preaching. The evaluation group constantly works to interpret the interviews in relation to the preaching. When the event is concluded, the whole congregation will reflect on what has been happening to them and what it means for their future. Of course, the pastor will reflect on what he or she has learned about preaching for healing. At many different levels there is an ongoing process of interpretation.

We have already emphasized that such events require continuing disciplined study. When the event is concluded, it must be written and interpreted. It seems appropriate to the community-formational process that the final write-up be shared with those who helped carry it out. Again, the relationships within the congregation are foundational to what is learned.

Students and faculty can then review what has happened during the course of the ministry event. Perhaps students and faculty can meet during the course of the event. They certainly must meet following the event. Together they review the report and reflect on it in terms of the student as they experience her or him within their own D.Min. community. Possibly, they will ask the student to preach to them so that they might experience firsthand what the student has learned. The argument is often made that preaching to fellow students is unreal and useless. Preaching is never unreal if it is more than an exercise, and if it is addressed directly to the persons present. Just as persons in the congregation can reflect on and help interpret the meaning of preaching, so also can students preach genuinely to fellow students and faculty.

One of the inherent dilemmas of a limited ministry event is that while it aims at ministry, it is also a research project. The purpose of research is to give careful attention to observed data as well as careful attention to the logic of proving or disproving a hypothesis. Research is characteristically objective; it tends to detach persons from the process.

We believe that research methods should never overcome the basic ministerial purpose of a ministry event. The effect of observation must therefore be carefully considered. If observation stands in the way of community formation, then the observation must be altered. Often, the opposite is true. In the example above, the evaluation group assisted the pastor in observation. Very likely, the regular meetings of the evaluation group with the pastor and the ongoing discussion of preaching will actually enhance the significance of preaching in that congregation. In that case, the observational method contributes to ministry. Should the observational method become so refined or intrusive that it interferes with the preaching or the healing, then the method must be modified or abandoned. A ministry event is knowledge in the service of ministry and not the other way around.

As we have described them, limited ministry events must demonstrate an evident relevance, a discernible movement toward community formation. Exegesis that does not result in effective preaching or more significant pastoral care, to cite only two instances, is ruled out. But does this not bind ministry to an immediate relevance? The answer is that a Doctor of Ministry program should feature a link between study of the tradition and responsible and discerning engagement in the present situation. The study of the tradition may be eminently worthwhile in itself. Indeed, it may be that theological training should give more attention to the study of Scripture and history. However, the church also needs persons who are able to act helpfully out of convictions shaped in the tradition. Such a link between growing understanding of the tradition and present community formation and interpretation is worthy of educational effort. The Doctor of Ministry degree keeps an eye on actual ministry, which includes a strong program of scholarship as such scholarship touches the formation of community. Other programs, e.g., the Doctor of Theology, feature study of the tradition without requiring ministerial relevance. However, such programs run the risk of losing the appropriate relationship of theology to actual relationships and communities.

A Manifesto for Ministry Education

The world desperately needs communities that are committed to the overcoming of the alienating, mechanizing, pluralizing tendencies of modern life. The world needs communities that are committed to overcoming the walls that separate the privileged and the underprivileged, the well fed and the hungry, the secure and the reviled, those with hope and those without hope. The church has for thousands of years announced that such human alienation is being overcome, and the church has sought in its life to embody the deepening of community that is more creative, more just, more intimate, and more faithful. Such interpretation and effort to embody a new spirit of community is the heart of ministry.

Seminaries are committed to training persons who can become leaders in the ministry of the church. The seminary does not contribute to ministry by simply talking about theology or "doing theology." What is needed are communities of faithfulness and commitment which are in touch with the Christian tradition and with present possibilities, communities which search for the truth that is already being shaped in living relationships. If seminaries are to prepare persons to engage in such ministry, they must themselves, at least in a provisional way, be such communities.

Seminaries teach ministry best when they become a community-forming reality, when preaching is genuine and when teaching is related to actual present relationships, when seminary administration is an occasion of learning together with students. The whole set of institutional relationships of the seminary becomes the primary teaching resource. It is in reaching for justice, and interpreting the effort, that the seminary teaches persons who can encourage justice in other settings. The seminary has a special vocation to study, and, remaining true to that vocation, to teach the student to assist other communities to remain true to their vocations.

If ministry is community formation and interpretation, then seminaries can train persons who are able to give helpful leadership to congregations by engaging them in the community formation and interpretation of seminary life. What is needed is for Christ to be embodied among us, whether that be at the level of preparation or of assignment. Whether in student life, the degree programs, faculty research, or finance, the actual practices and relationships of the seminary are a primary teaching resource.

In a clandestine seminary during the Nazi period in

Germany, Dietrich Bonhoeffer wrote of seminary life in *Life Together.*[9] He spoke of the way that life together springs from common faith and is shaped by worship and work rituals through the day. To drink deeply of such community is to become prepared to be a minister of Christ in other communities. It is time for seminaries to turn to those resources in their midst that give the greatest vitality to preparation for ministry.

Notes and References

Introduction

1. In focusing on community formation as the proper context of practical theology we side with Bonhoeffer's thesis in *Communio Sanctorium,* and with Karl Barth's focus on God's Word as a community-forming reality. Here is the significance of Barth's entitling his work in systematic theology as "church dogmatics."

2. Aquinas understood practical theology to be the application of the first principles of ethics to the particularity of experience. In his account of the moral syllogism, when the reasonable principles of ethics encounter particular circumstances, then a moral conclusion will be drawn.

3. A more detailed description of the practical theology discussion will follow in chapter 2. Several recent publications have drawn out the major issues in this discussion: Don S. Browning, ed., *Practical Theology: The Emerging Field in Theology, Church, and World* (New York: Harper & Row, 1982); Edward Farley, *Theologia: The Fragmentation and Unity of Theological Education* (Philadelphia: Fortress Press, 1983). David Tracy is working on the third volume of a set which includes foundational theology, systematic theology, and practical theology. We understand our work to be a part of this dialogue.

4. John J. Ansbro, *Martin Luther King: The Making of a Mind* (Maryknoll, N.Y.: Orbis Books, 1982).

5. The concept of community lifts out many of the themes of the kingdom of God. The kingdom is the realm of God's rule. For individuals to be related to the kingdom is to be joined together with other persons. The kingdom of God is more nearly among us than within us. The corollary to the kingdom of God is the people of God. Therefore, the kingdom is the community-forming reality of our lives. In view of the centrality of the kingdom in Jesus' preaching in the Synoptic Gospels, it is surprising that the kingdom has not been more central to practical theology. Our focus on community points to the kingdom. See Norman Perrin, *The Kingdom of God in the Teaching of Jesus,* (Philadelphia: Westminster Press, 1963); *Jesus and the Language of the Kingdom,* (Philadelphia: Fortress Press, 1976).

6. Community as we see it refers to a set of hypotheses, patterns of interaction, common belief, and a vision of new possibility. It therefore has both an empirical and visional polarity. We are not assuming that the church community as it exists is unflawed. Our plea is for a new sense of community, but this very sense includes both grace and judgment. Tillich has a similar vision of a theonomous community that time and again overcomes the separateness of existence, *Systematic Theology,* vol. 3 (Chicago: University of Chicago Press, 1963), pp. 245 ff. We note that liberation theologians have a similar concern for community as the basis for renewal of the church and the society, e.g., Jose Miguez Bonino, *Doing Theology in a Revolutionary Situation* (Philadelphia: Fortress Press, 1975). One who is trying to draw out the implications of liberation theology for practical theology is Thomas Groome, *Christian Religious Education* (New York: Harper & Row, 1980).

7. Several recent books by U.S. theologians are responding to liberation theology and to the political theologies of J. B. Metz and others. See Matthew L. Lamb, *Solidarity with Victims: Toward a Theology of Social Transformation* (New York: Crossroad Publishing Co., 1982); John B. Cobb, Jr., *Process Theology as Political Theology* (Philadelphia: Westminster Press, 1982); Schubert M. Ogden, *The Point of Christology* (New York: Harper & Row, 1982).

8. Edward Farley, *Ecclesial Reflection: An Anatomy of Theological Method* (Philadelphia: Fortress Press, 1982).

9. "Pluralism" has several meanings within the theological community. It can refer to the lack of a coherent world view or philosophy in Western culture, to a positivism that denies the possibility of the unity of the sciences, to the variety of theological viewpoints, to the sub-disciplines within theology, or to the variety of value-orientations within local communities of faith. The various meanings of pluralism have been worked out in several places and we are indebted to these discussions. We believe that pluralism is an accurate description of the fragmentation and disunity which is found at all levels of discussion and shared life. See David Tracy, *Blessed Rage for Order: The New Pluralism in Theology* (New York: Seabury Press, 1979); John B. Cobb, Jr., *Christ in a Pluralistic Age* (Philadelphia: Westminster Press, 1975); Don S. Browning, *Pluralism and Personality: William James and Some Contemporary Cultures of Psychology* (Lewisburg, Pa.: Bucknell University Press, 1980).

10. Several major studies have explored the guiding images of ministry and have tried to provide unity in the midst of the sub-disciplines. The Association of Theological Schools has been most active in promoting such studies of ministry. Recently, David S. Schuller et al., eds., *Ministry in America* (New York: Harper & Row, 1980). During the fifties, a study resulted in several books: H. Richard Niebuhr and others, *The Purpose of the Church and Its Ministry* (New York: Harper & Row, 1956); and H. Richard Niebuhr and Daniel Day Williams, eds., *The Ministry in Historical Perspective* (New York: Harper & Row, 1956).

11. Farley, *Theologia*, pp. 175-76.

12. The various historical critical methods of interpretation have attempted to locate a biblical text within its historical setting. Studies of the circumstances of the writing of the texts, the intention of the author, the oral background to a text, the oral form in which it arose, the *Sitz im Leben* (Bultmann), have illuminated texts in terms of the particular communities in which they arose. Then came redaction criticism which traced the changing interpretation of the same text. More

recently redaction criticism has focused in canon criticism which is an effort to see how a text functioned in the formation of the canon. Canon criticism moves toward understanding how an earlier community believed a text to be God's special message. See Brevard Childs, *Introduction to the Old Testament as Scripture* (Philadelphia: Fortress Press, 1979); James A. Sanders, *Torah and Canon* (Philadelphia: Fortress Press, 1972); Walter Brueggemann, *The Creative Word* (Philadelphia: Fortress Press, 1982).

13. David Tracy, "A Thought-Project: Particular Classics, Public Religion in the American Tradition"; "Theological Interpretation of the Bible Today" (Manuscripts).

14. Phyllis Trible, *God and the Rhetoric of Sexuality* (Philadelphia: Fortress Press, 1978), p. 3; Brueggemann, *The Creative Word.*

15. Tracy, "A Thought-Project."

16. Groome, *Christian Religious Education,* p. 186. This is also what we understand as "subversive memory" as described by J. B. Metz, *Faith in History and Society* (New York: Seabury Press, 1980), p. 90.

17. This point has been well made by the Latin American theologians and by the European political theologians. See Gustavo Gutierrez, *A Theology of Liberation* (Maryknoll, N.Y.: Orbis Books, 1973), as an example of the Latin American theologians. See Johann B. Metz, *The Emergent Church: The Future of Christianity in a Post-Bourgeois World* (New York: Crossroad Publishing Co., 1981), as an example of European political theology. Both emphasize the radical political nature of the gospel in its own time and in our time and the need to shift the context of theology from the privileged, dominant societies to the poor and dispossessed.

18. Examples of North American theologies of liberation are James Cone, *God of the Oppressed* (New York: Seabury Press, 1978), and Rosemary Ruether, *The Radical Kingdom* (Ramsey, N.J.: Paulist Press, 1975).

19. Norman Gottwald, *The Tribes of Yahweh: A Sociology of the Religion of Liberated Israel* (Maryknoll, N.Y.: Orbis Books, 1979).

20. On the discussion of language as metaphorical and ambiguous, see Charles E. Winquist, *Practical Hermeneutics* (Chico, Calif.: Scholars Press, 1979), pp. 31 ff. See also Bernard E. Meland, *Fallible Forms and Symbols* (Philadelphia: Fortress Press, 1976); Tillich, *Systematic Theology,* vol. 1, pp. 239 ff. See also Paul Ricoeur, "Metaphor and the Central Problem of Hermeneutics," in *Hermeneutics and the Human Sciences* (New York: Cambridge University Press, 1981), pp. 165 ff.; and Tracy, "Religious Language in the New Testament," in *Blessed Rage for Order,* pp. 119 ff.

21. We refer here to the discussion about the locus of practical theology as public and universal in character or as located in the mission of the church. See Browning, *Practical Theology,* pp. 10 ff, 164 ff. See also Groome, *Christian Religious Education,* pp. 184 ff.

2. Types of Practical Theology

1. We wish to acknowledge the corporate nature of these considerations. At Bethany Seminary, as in other theological schools, we try to function as a community of searchers for truth. By the time any idea is written down, it is already the product of many minds because of the discussions we have had together. We acknowledge our dependence on that dialogue for this chapter, especially to Lauree Hersch Meyer and Graydon Snyder. Without their input, this material would not have been written.

2. See Max Weber, *Methodology of the Social Sciences* (New York: Free Press, 1949).

3. Matthew L. Lamb, ed., *Creativity and Method: Studies in Honor of Rev. Bernard Lonergan* (Milwaukee, Wis.: Marquette University Press, 1981), pp. 53-77.

4. *Pastoral Psychology,* February 1950, p. 5.

5. James Lapsley, "Practical Theology and Pastoral Care," in *Practical Theology,* p. 169.

6. Ibid., p. 170.

7. Don S. Browning, "Pastoral Theology in a Pluralistic Age," in *Practical Theology,* p. 192.

8. Ibid., p. 191.

9. David Tracy, "Foundations of Practical Theology," in *Practical Theology*, p. 61.

10. Don S. Browning, "Preface to a Practical Theology of Aging," in *Toward a Theology of Aging*, ed. Seward Hiltner (New York: Human Sciences Press, 1975), pp. 152-53; see also Tracy, *Practical Theology*, p. 3.

11. Don S. Browning, "Toward a Practical Theology of Care," *Union Seminary Quarterly Review*, Winter-Spring, 1981, p. 161.

12. Ibid., p. 159.

13. Tracy, *Practical Theology*, p. 78.

14. Browning, "Introduction," in *Practical Theology*, p. 15.

15. Ibid., p. 11.

16. James Fowler, "Practical Theology and the Shaping of Christian Lives," in *Practical Theology*, p. 152.

17. Ibid., p. 149.

18. Ibid.

19. Thomas Ogletree, "Dimensions of Practical Theology: Meaning, Action, Self," in *Practical Theology*, p. 86.

20. Ibid., p. 90.

21. Browning, *Practical Theology*, p. 14.

22. Fowler, *Practical Theology*, p. 149.

23. Ibid., p. 164.

24. Ibid., pp. 164-65.

25. The confessional method seeks to uncover its own subservience to economic and political forces. However, it allows contemporary experience to criticize the tradition. Contemporary philosophy and science can open new understanding of the tradition so long as the contemporary norms are not allowed to replace the confessional norm. Karl Barth's *Church Dogmatics* is the classic formulation of the confessional method. Barth accepts historical and critical examination of the tradition but works constantly to keep an alien philosophical or theological norm from intruding upon the Christian story.

26. Leander Keck, "Toward a Theology of Rhetoric/ Preaching," in *Practical Theology*, p. 134.

27. John Howard Yoder, *The Politics of Jesus* (Grand Rapids: Wm. B. Eerdmans Publishing Co., 1972), p. 18 (footnote).

28. Lewis Mudge (Private conversation, October 11, 1982).

29. Graydon Snyder, "Theological Education from a Free Church Perspective," *Theological Education,* Spring, 1981, p. 176.

30. Groome, *Christian Religious Education,* p. 184.

31. For a contemporary statement of the Lutheran ethic, see Paul Tillich, *Love, Power, and Justice* (New York: Oxford University Press, 1960).

32. Troeltsch argues that the Calvinist concern for the purity of the congregation has some affinity to the Anabaptists, *The Social Teaching of the Christian Churches,* vol. 2 (New York: Macmillan, 1956), pp. 593 ff.

33. For a recent Roman Catholic effort in this direction see the bishops' pastoral letter on the arms race.

34. Farley, in *Practical Theology,* pp. 38-39.

35. Lewis Mudge, "The Mind of the Church" (Paper from University of Chicago Seminar, 1981), p. 3.

36. Ibid., p. 28.

37. Ibid., p. 13.

38. David C. Steinmetz, "The Protestant Minister and the Teaching Office of the Church," *Theological Education,* Spring, 1983, p. 47.

39. John B. Cobb, Jr., "Authority and Theology in Ecumenical Protestantism," *Theological Education,* Spring, 1983, pp. 33-44.

40. Snyder, "Theological Education from a Free Church Perspective," p. 175.

3. A Method for Practical Theology

1. Fowler, *Practical Theology,* p. 149.

2. Tracy, *Blessed Rage for Order,* p. 45 ff.

3. For a fuller description of a narrative assessment as the basis for practical decision, see James M. Gustafson, *Ethics*

from a Theocentric Perspective (Chicago: University of Chicago Press, 1981).

4. Hegel is usually given credit for discovering the radical socio-historical nature of experience. More recently Wilhelm Dilthey and Ernst Troeltsch have developed the conception. Process theology has joined with historicist theology to magnify the emphasis.

5. See H. Richard Niebuhr, *The Responsible Self*, and George Herbert Mead, *Mind, Self, and Society* (Chicago: University of Chicago Press, 1967).

6. For a discussion of the concept "praxis" see Groome, *Christian Religious Education*, pp. 152-83.

7. Bernard E. Meland, ed., *The Future of Empirical Theology*, (Chicago: University of Chicago Press, 1969), pp. 8, 176.

8. Ibid., pp. 12, 13.

9. Ibid., p. 290.

10. Ibid., pp. 302, 296.

11. Ibid., pp. 301-2.

12. Ibid., p. 301

13. Ibid., p. 292.

14. Here, again, we refer to the character of intentionality in perception as that which has been investigated by writers such as Marx, Weber, Dilthey, Husserl, Schutz, Habermas, and others.

15. Winquist, *Practical Hermeneutics*, p. 31.

16. Meland, *The Future of Empirical Theology*, pp. 7, 8.

17. Groome, *Christian Religious Education*, p. 170.

18. Paul Ricoeur, *The Philosophy of Paul Ricoeur* (Boston: Beacon Press, 1978), p. 89.

19. Browning, *Practical Theology*, p. 62.

20. James Sanders, "The Bible as Canon," *Christian Century*, December 2, 1981, pp. 1250-55.

21. Browning, *Practical Theology*, p. 150.

22. Tracy, *Blessed Rage for Order*, pp. 34, 47.

23. Ibid., p. 52.

24. Meland, *The Future of Empirical Theology*, p. 177.

25. Meland, *Fallible Forms and Symbols*, p. 144.

26. Meland, *The Future of Empirical Theology*, p. 180.

27. Meland, *Fallible Forms and Symbols.*

28. Ricoeur, *The Philosophy of Paul Ricoeur,* p. 98.

29. Arthur J. Dyck, "Moral Requiredness: Bridging the Gap Between 'Ought' and 'Is,' " *Journal of Religious Ethics, Part I,* Fall, 1978, pp. 293-318; *Part II,* Spring, 1981, pp. 131-50.

30. Mead, *Mind, Self, and Society.*

31. Winquist, *Practical Hermeneutics,* pp. 5, 6, 31, 27, 31-32, 41, 42.

32. Something such as this seems to be about what Gustafson means in his book, *Ethics from a Theocentric Perspective.*

33. Alfred North Whitehead, *Process and Reality* (New York: Free Press, 1978), pp. 4-6.

34. James M. Gustafson, *Theology and Christian Ethics* (New York: Pilgrim Press, 1974).

35. Don S. Browning, *Religious Ethics and Pastoral Care* (Philadelphia: Fortress Press, 1983), pp. 53-71.

36. Groome, *Christian Religious Education,* pp. 184 ff.

37. Rodney Hunter, "The Future of Pastoral Theology," *Pastoral Psychology,* Fall, 1980, pp. 65, 66.

38. Ibid., p. 65.

39. Ibid.

4. Guidelines for the Practice of Ministry

1. Wayne Judd, "The Equipment of the Saints: A Vision for Ministry" (Doctor of Ministry Project, Bethany Theological Seminary, 1977).

2. Ibid., p. 100.

3. Douglas R. Loving, "Spiritual Growth: An Intentional Strategy for the Local Church" (Doctor of Ministry Project, Bethany Theological Seminary, 1979).

4. Ibid., p. 50.

5. Fred Bernhard, "Hospitality: The Essence of the Church's Life and Witness" (Doctor of Ministry Project, Bethany Theological Seminary, 1982).

6. Chris Michael, "Sermons for City Sheep" (Confidential

Doctor of Ministry Learning Unit, Bethany Theological Seminary, 1982).

7. Eric C. Stumpf, "A Local Diaconate for a Lutheran Parish" (Doctor of Ministry Project, Bethany Theological Seminary, 1980).

8. Ibid., p. 26.

9. Thomas Wilson, "The Last Days of the Church" (Doctor of Ministry Project, Bethany Theological Seminary, 1979).

5. Community Formation as the Task of Ministry

1. James and Evelyn Whitehead, *Community of Faith* (New York: Seabury Press, 1982), pp. 21-33.

2. Daniel D. Williams, *The Spirit and Forms of Love* (New York: Harper & Row, 1968), p. 146.

3. Ibid., p. 153.

4. The understanding of life as a tension between unity and diversity, the one and the many, has been well developed in Process Theology. The following are key articles in the development of this understanding: Williams, *The Spirit and the Forms of Love;* Bernard M. Loomer, "Two Kinds of Power," *Criterion,* 15 (1976); Bernard M. Loomer, "The Free and Relational Self," in *Belief and Ethics,* eds. W. W. Schroeder and Gibson Winter (Center for the Scientific Study of Religion, 1978); see also Tillich, *Systematic Theology,* vol. 1, pp. 174 ff. The ontological polarities of individualization and participation are similar.

5. Daniel D. Williams, "God and Time," *South East Asia Journal of Theology,* January, 1961, p. 14.

6. "Process of interaction" is a coined term which draws on the process philosophy of A. N. Whitehead and the social psychology of George Herbert Mead. Williams refers to Whitehead's view of reality as a "process of becoming" within a social network; Williams, "God and Time," p. 14. Mead refers to this process of interaction on the human level as a "conversation of gestures" which is the context for the development of community; Mead, *Mind, Self, and Society,*

p. 7. See also Loomer, "The Free and Relational Self," p. 71.

7. We refer here to the discussion in ethics and theology about story as the genre that contains the living metaphors for particular communities. Alasdair MacIntyre, *After Virtue* (Notre Dame, Ind.: University of Notre Dame Press, 1981); Stanley Hauerwas, *A Community of Character,* (Notre Dame, Ind.: University of Notre Dame Press, 1981); Gordon D. Kaufman, *The Theological Imagination* (Philadelphia: Westminster Press, 1981); Warren Groff, *Story Time,* (Elgin, Ill.: Brethren Press, 1974); Eugene F. Roop, *Living the Biblical Story* (Nashville: Abingdon Press, 1979).

8. Delwin Brown et al., ed., *Process Philosophy and Christian Thought* (Indianapolis, Ind.: Bobbs-Merrill Co., 1971), p. 8.

9. John Cobb and David Griffin, *Process Theology* (Philadelphia: Westminster Press, 1976), pp. 22 ff.

10. Stanley Hauerwas, *Vision and Virtue* (Notre Dame, Ind.: University of Notre Dame Press, 1981), pp. 68-92.

11. Charles Hartshorne, *The Divine Relativity* (New Haven: Yale University Press, 1948).

12. The socio-political context has been well described as a web of relationships by Bernard Loomer in "The Size of God" (in authors' possession in manuscript form).

13. This line of argument has been well represented by Brueggemann in *The Creative Word,* pp. 41 ff.

14. We are indebted here to the development of a social psychology which understands reality in terms of interacting dynamic systems. Various influences from anthropology, cybernetics, and family studies in schizophrenia and delinquency have come together in some suggestive ideas about the nature of human interaction in community. Many of the seminal articles have been collected in a volume edited by Paul Watzlawick and John Weakland, *The Interactional View* (New York: W. W. Norton & Co., 1977). Other key authors in this field include Gregory Bateson, Von Bertalanffy, Jay Haley. A recent summary of the literature has been done by Lynn Hoffman in *Foundations of Family Therapy* (New York: Basic Books, 1981). See also the journal, *Family Process.*

15. The tension between deep sensitivity to the past and the

intrusion of novelty from outside a system is well discussed in Process Theology. The debate is clearly focused in Meland, *The Future of Empirical Theology.* Meland has further developed his ideas about appreciative awareness in *Fallible Forms and Symbols.* The need for a transcendent source of "novelty" is argued by Cobb and Griffin, *Process Theology,* p. 28.

16. Boundaries and hierarchy are fairly common constructs in the field of family systems. Both the clinical and theoretical aspects of this understanding of human interaction are being developed in several places. We have been most deeply influenced by Salvador Minuchin, *Families and Family Therapy* (Cambridge, Mass.: Harvard University Press, 1974), and other works; Jay Haley, *Problem-Solving Therapy* (San Francisco: Jossey-Bass, 1976), and other works: Murray Bowen, *Family Therapy in Clinical Practice* (New York: Jason Aronson, 1978); Elizabeth Carter and Monica McGoldrick eds., *The Family Life Cycle* (New York: Halsted Press, 1980).

17. Our views of intimacy are most influenced by the psychoanalytic tradition, including Freud, Erikson, and ego psychology, especially Margaret Mahler et al., *The Psychological Birth of the Human Infant* (New York: Basic Books, 1975); Otto Kernberg, *Internal World and External Reality* (New York: Jason Aronson, 1980); Althea Horner, *Object Relations and the Developing Ego in Therapy* (New York: Jason Aronson, 1979). We are also interested in the feminist discussion of intimacy and gender identity. See Nancy Chodorow, *The Reproduction of Mothering* (Berkeley: University of California Press, 1978), and Jane Gallop, *The Daughter's Seduction* (Ithaca: Cornell University Press, 1982).

18. We believe that the meaning level of personal and community life is helpfully developed in the work of Jean Piaget and his students in the field of moral and faith development. See especially Lawrence Kohlberg, *The Philosophy of Moral Development* (New York: Harper & Row, 1981); Robert Kegan, *The Evolving Self* (Cambridge, Mass.: Harvard University Press, 1982); James Fowler, *Stages of Faith* (New York: Harper & Row, 1981). We also find the

feminist critique very helpful. See Carol Gilligan, *In a Different Voice* (Cambridge, Mass.: Harvard University Press, 1982).

6. The Challenge to Ministry Education

1. A recent commentator on seminary education who has received much attention is Farley, *Theologia.*

2. We are not arguing that a seminary is a fully recognized congregation. It is, rather, a community of faith with ecclesial significance. Its official congregational status will depend on the church order in the communion(s) to which it is related. Questions about celebration of liturgy must be explored in terms of church order, but there, again, the actual institutional relationships thereby become a primary teaching resource.

3. For an extended discussion of shared praxis, see Groome, *Christian Religious Education.*

4. The contrast between a fourfold traditional curriculum and a newer threefold curriculum is drawn by Farley, *Theologia.*

5. Ibid. pp. 29 ff.

6. For students to participate in community functions, they must be qualified to carry the function in question. Their participation must therefore be gauged according to what they are genuinely able to contribute or grow into. Just being there they can consider the lure of God's will for themselves in the setting.

7. Auburn and Hartford Seminaries jointly are currently engaged in a study of the problems of the Doctor of Minister degree.

8. See the Association of Theological Schools, *Procedures, Standards, and Criteria for Membership,* Bulletin 35, part 3, pp. 31 ff.

9. Dietrich Bonhoeffer, *Life Together* (New York: Harper & Row, 1954).

Index

Administration, 92-98, 105-8
Anabaptists, 109
Anselm, 90
Aquinas, Thomas, 10
Authority, 16, 57

Barth, Karl, 83
Bellah, Robert, 40
Benedictines, 109
Bethany Theological Seminary, 175, 180
Bible, 16, 22, 66, 137
Browning, Don, 8, 43, 46, 48, 49, 50, 82, 94, 97

Calvin, John, 54
Christian tradition, 82
Church, 14, 33, 53-59
  ecumenical, 21
  growth, 108-10
Church of the Brethren, 36
Classic(al), 23
Cobb, John, 57
Community, 126-46

Christian community, 12, 13
faith community, 9, 48
living community, 64
Confessional method, 50-59, 86-91
Congregation, 100-125, 148
Correlation, 43-50, 62, 65, 82-86
Creativity, 138-40
Critical, 31-32, 62-63, 77-82, 91-92

Description, 66, 70-77, 95
Diaconate, deacons, 114-16
Dilthey, Wilhelm, 68
Discipleship, 12, 25
Doctor of Ministry, 160-68
Durkheim, Emile, 40

Ecclesial, 55
Education, theological, 29, 147-70

Empirical, 66-69, 73, 87
Enlightenment, 10
Ethics, 43
Evangelism, 108-10
Existential, existentialism, 47
Experience
  human, 64-65
  lived, 70-81

Faith, 144-45
Farley, Edward, 55, 58, 158
Feminism, 70, 76
Field education, 151-52
Formation, 62, 66
Fosdick, H. E., 112
Fowler, James, 47, 49, 50, 62, 84
Freud, Sigmund, 32, 33, 40

God, 134-36, 141
Groome, Thomas, 53, 95
Guidelines, 92-97, 100
Gustafson, James, 93-95, 97

Habermas, Jurgen, 81, 91
Hartshorne, Charles, 135
Hegel, G. F., 32
Hermeneutics, 82-86
Hiltner, Seward, 43
Hospitality, 108-10,
Howe, Reuel, 103
Hume, David, 10
Hunger, 14

Hunter, Rodney, 95-97
Husserl, Edmund, 68

Interaction, 12, 64, 129-31
Interpretation, 9, 65-66, 86-91
Intimacy, 142-44

Jesus, 105, 109, 141
Justice, 140-41

Kant, Immanuel, 32, 33
Keck, Leander, 51
Kingdom, 12

Language, 24-25
  empirical, 26, 64, 66-69, 87, 93
  metaphorical, 24-25
  phenomenologial, 67, 80
Lapsley, James, 39
Larson, Bruce, 106
Latin America, 15, 23, 37
Leadership, 18
  pastoral, 18, 166
  professional, 19-20, 40
  religious, 13
  specialized, 19-20, 29, 39
Liberation theology, 29, 37, 79, 136
Locke, John, 80
Luther, Martin, 53, 57, 101, 114, 140
Lutheran, 114-16

Marx, Karl, 32, 34
McCann, Dennis P., 46
Mead, George Herbert, 132-33
Meaning, 62, 86-91
Meland, Bernard, 70-72, 80, 87-88
Miller, Donald Earl, 40
Miller, Keith, 106
Mudge, Lewis, 52-53, 56

Niebuhr, H. Richard, 37
Nietzsche, F., 32
Normative, 65-66, 95

Ogletree, Thomas, 47-48
Oppressed, 14, 23, 33, 92
Otto, Rudolph, 69

Pastoral care, 103-5, 114-16
Pastoral Psychology, 38
Phenomenology, 68-69
Pietism, 101, 115
Planning, 92-97, 100
Pluralism, 17, 29, 44, 58
Poor, 14, 15
Poverty, 33, 79
Practice, 100-102
Pragmatic, 93
Praxis, 29, 34, 48, 53, 65, 95
Preaching, 51, 111-13
Process theology, 67
Psychoanalysis, 81
Public, 34, 45, 48

Racial change, 116-18
Reformation, 114
Ricoeur, Paul, 56, 88
Roman Catholic, 54, 57, 101

Schleiermacher, Friedrich, 47, 68
Science, 31, 36, 38
Scriptures
  Genesis 1:10, 128
  Jeremiah 11:4, 128
  Gospel of Matthew, 109
  Matthew 20:28, 11
  Matthew 25:36, 103
  John 15:5, 128
  Galatians 6:10, 110
  Ephesians 4:11-12, 103, 124
  I Timothy 3, 114
  II Timothy 2, 114
  Hebrews 11:16, 113
  Revelation 21:2, 113
Seminary curriculum, 147-70
Servanthood, 12
Snyder, Graydon, 53, 58
Social science, 37, 39
Society, 33, 50
Specialization, 147-48
Spiritual growth, 105-8
Steinmetz, David, 57

Theological education, 29, 147-70
Theology

as a discipline, 9, 22-26, 29, 64, 147-48
as interpretation, 10, 12, 13
philosophical, 85
reflection, 11, 62-64
systematic, 29
Theory, 48, 95
Therapy, 78
Third World, 15
Tillich, Paul, 42, 66, 69, 90
Tracy, David, 43-44, 47, 62, 82, 83, 85
Transformation, 50, 59
Troeltsch, Ernst, 34, 40, 41, 54, 55, 58, 68

Turner, Victor, 83
Types, ideal, 30-31, 34

Urban ministry, 111-13

Value, 62, 86-91

Weber, Max, 30-31, 34, 40
Wesley, John, 105
Whitehead, A. N., 66, 93
Williams, D. D., 43, 67-68, 86
Winquist, Charles, 89-90

Yoder, John Howard, 51-52

p.69 – 6 components or steps in
Practical Theology

p.100 – summary of chapters 2+3